FLOWERS IN HELL
AN INVESTIGATION INTO WOMEN AND CRIME

Barney Bardsley is a freelance journalist, writer and editor for various radical magazines in London, specialising in theatre and in contemporary literature. She was a collective member of the *Leveller* magazine and of Sheba Feminist Publishers, and edited the books and arts pages of *Tribune* from 1984 to 1986. She is currently training in dance. *Flowers in Hell* is Barney Bardsley's first book.

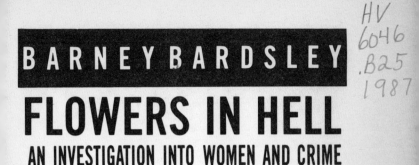

BARNEY BARDSLEY

FLOWERS IN HELL
AN INVESTIGATION INTO WOMEN AND CRIME

PANDORA

London and New York

First published in 1987 by Pandora Press
(Routledge & Kegan Paul Ltd)
11 New Fetter Lane, London EC4P 4EE

Published in the USA by Pandora Press
(Routledge & Kegan Paul Inc.)
in association with Methuen Inc.
29 West 35th Street, New York, NY 10001

Set in 10/12pt Bembo
by Witwell Limited
and printed in Great Britain
by The Guernsey Press Co. Ltd
Guernsey, Channel Islands

Library of Congress Cataloging in Publication Data

Bardsley, Barney.
  Flowers in hell.

  Bibliography: p.
  Includes index.
  1. Female offenders–Great Britain.   I. Title.
HV6046.B25   1987   364.3'74'0941   87-8914

British Library CIP Data also available
ISBN 0-86358-197-8 (p)
     0-86358-065-3 (c)

DEDICATION

For Carol, the 'wild, flying dove'. Shortly after talking to me with a fearless optimism about her 'criminal' past, and her hopeful future, Carol died – too young, too bright, too precious. Anything good in this book is for her.

CONTENTS

ACKNOWLEDGMENTS

First of all, love and thanks to the women who shared their often painful, sometimes hilarious criminal experiences with me. They are incognito here – but well remembered. All names in the main text have been changed unless first *and* surnames have been given in full.

Thanks also to those working within the penal system who talked to me, particularly to Mr J. Greenhill of the Inner London Magistrates Court, who tells me he has never been acknowledged in a book before, and who deserves it here – for spending a whole afternoon explaining the intricacies of the British legal system to me, and making me realise that there are people with integrity working in the courts.

Special thanks to Jenny Hicks of Clean Break Theatre and Chris Tchaikovsky of Women in Prison, who have been so supportive, patient, and endlessly helpful.

And finally, personal thanks to my mum and dad for approving of everything I do; to Liz and Martha Mellon for being a fabulous source of humour and strength during the time when I thought this book was totally beyond me; to Gered and Spotty Dog for being old and treasured pals; to Brigid McConville for persuading me that writing

books was really not that big a deal!; to Douglas Hill for setting m
on my writing and editing feet at *Tribune*; and to Andi for teaching m
how to dance, when the words refused to come.

'There we were, my sister and I, as vulnerable as flowers in hell.'
Quoted from the personal diaries of June and Jennifer Gibbons,
sent to Broadmoor in 1983, in *The Silent Twins*, Marjorie Wallace
(Chatto & Windus, 1986).

'You're caught up in a conflict of what's goin' on outside you, and
what's goin' on inside. To decide what to do for the best is just
totally impossible. Something suffers in the end. And I went down
to prison… Deep inside I'm scared, but I've got great courage as
well. I'll just shut my eyes and dive in… I'm gonna fuckin' swim.
I'm not gonna allow myself to drown.' *Carol*

INTRODUCTION

I have come to the subject of crime not as an 'expert', full of theory and conviction, but as someone who simply wanted to find out: <u>why do women break the law</u>? Many times I have felt a strong desire to smash something from anger, to cheat and to steal from impoverishment, to create fearsome public disturbances out of sheer bloody-mindedness. But something powerful has always held me back: nice girls don't. ...And I didn't. But that has not stopped me feeling a strong affinity for those women who *do* have the nerve to commit crime, to transgress those unspoken barriers of saintly femininity, and be *bad*.

So I am grateful to Philippa Brewster, my editor, for having faith enough in my writing to commission this book – my first – on such a complex subject. It is very easy, when researching, to become dragged down in all the literature available. Crime and the motivation behind it has become a highly sophisticated area of study for academics and students, and the 'criminology' section of large libraries will furnish you with every conceivable theory under the sun as to what this 'criminal' creature is, and how s/he should be contained. Frankly, most of this material bored and appalled me.

With a mixture of meaningless statistics and stereotyping (picked up by the media and used daily to sell newspapers), the writers did little but mystify human behaviour into a web of highly intricate and obscure pathologies. They usually claimed to have interviewed hundreds of criminals – but they rarely seemed to have *listened* properly to any of them. Painful human experience was transformed into clinical observation, all passions squeezed dry.

There are, of course, honourable exceptions to this, and two different kinds of book did help me a lot: those by the new generation of feminist criminologists, like Pat Carlen, who takes to task all the old sexist theories about women and crime with wit and precision, to present a view which takes into account vital questions of class and culture; and the first-hand accounts by women ex-prisoners, like Chris Tchaikovsky and Josie O'Dwyer, whose personal experiences speak with more integrity and impact than volumes of academic research. I wanted my book to have the fierceness of those 'own stories' and the breadth of scope which coming in as an outsider would give me. Most of all I wanted to talk to criminal women themselves. Their voices are crucial to this book. It is written for them.

The long, sometimes tortured, sometimes hilarious conversations I have had with the contributors to *Flowers in Hell* – most of whom have been re-named in the book – have moved and educated me. If I had any notion before of criminal women as 'victims' it has now been wiped clean. The only appropriate word is 'survivor'. The intelligent insights they have offered me, on a political and personal level, will always stay with me. I have learned that women who break the law suffer terrible hardships in court, in prison and in outside society. They pay the price for breaking the code of acceptable female behaviour – and it is a high one. Sometimes I felt on the verge of breakdown, just listening to their stories – and one very lovely woman has in fact died since, a loss I feel as keenly as if I had known her for years. When you live on an emotional raw edge, as many of these women do, it takes its toll in spirit and flesh. But they rarely give in – not without a bloody good fight.

I started this book with only one question: why do women get involved in crime? Often, when male criminals are discussed, there is

a suggestion of masculine rebellion, but with women a more
image comes to mind, one of petty crime and of desperate, con
behaviour. I wanted to turn that notion on its head, and see if women
too, could be criminal rebels. There's no call for romantic falsehoods
– crime often means agony for those who commit it, and those who
suffer from it – but I found that women criminals are not the duffers
many may imagine them to be. It is wrong to underestimate them.

The first three chapters of the book look at reasons for women
breaking the law, treatment of female criminals by police and courts,
and the experience of prison. Chapters 4 and 5 examine stereotypes of
the criminal woman – the label of 'madness', and the cultural images
of men, women and crime on television, film and in literature. Finally
the sixth chapter looks at 'political crime'. What is it? And what are
its links to and differences from other types of crime committed by
women? Isn't *all* crime political?

Flowers in Hell is not meant to be just one more addition to the
criminological canon. What I want it to do instead is to make a world
too often hidden away by taboo accessible to a general readership; to
stop people from wagging their fingers, and turning their backs. It is
not any kind of apology for crime – people who are robbed,
mugged, defrauded suffer an inexcusable intimidation – but they can
only be *helped* by an attempt to understand why crime occurs. I have
talked to many 'non-criminal' women for the book, and their
comments appear alongside those of criminal women, to show how
false the division often is between the 'criminal' and the 'ordinary'
person. If, after reading this book, you no longer say 'Look at them,
ugh', but wonder instead whether 'That could be me...' then it will
have served some purpose.

CHAPTER 1

DID SHE

D... T?

I feel guilt
I feel guilt
Though I know I've done no wrong I feel guilt

I feel bad
I feel bad
Though I ain't done nothin' wrong I feel bad

I never lied to my lover
But if I did I would admit it
If I could get away with murder
I'd take my gun and I'd commit it

I never gave to the rich
I never stole from the poor
Like a curious child – give me more, more, more...

('Guilt' by Reynolds, *Broken English* album, Marianne Faithfull, Island
Records)

If there is one virtue Western society would love to confer on women, it is that of innocence. They have always been idealised as moral guardians – taking on guilt and responsibility for men's misdemeanours, but staying blameless and 'above reproach' themselves. If they have a part to play in crime – that most publicly despised and 'masculine' of human activities – then it is only as a passive vessel, a victim. A recent British government hoarding, produced as part of a massive crime prevention campaign, underlined this view by blowing up a huge image of a beautiful white woman, her eyes grey-green and vigilant. 'You're already well-equipped to prevent crime,' it pronounced. 'Don't let them get away with it.' The implication? That men commit crime, while women suffer, observe, and – hopefully – civilise them out of it.

Many non-criminal women share this view – and not just traditionally minded women. One diehard radical reckoned that 'men are natural twisters, naturally opportunist, and greedier than women. Men's golden times always involve the adrenalin running – games, conflicts, competition, war, revolution, pitting their wits and strength and ability against an adversary. With this background, they are more likely to break rules, manipulate the evidence, grab and snatch, commit crimes of all kinds.... Laws have been passed simply to civilise the males.... Women are not thought of as "criminal" because of this; the laws are just not aimed at them.'

But women *do* commit crime, of course. Their 'biological innocence' is a dangerous fiction. Yet even though this is public knowledge, the prevailing social view remains polarised between the 'passive' female and the 'active' male. When I started asking 'ordinary' women what images came into their heads when they thought of female crime, a rather feeble picture emerged (later replaced with a more realistic view, when their stereotypes were challenged). One woman conjured up 'desperate' losers, women with 'personality defects' – 'People who just don't stand a chance.' Another said, 'I think women commit crimes because they are very angry, bored, not feeling good in themselves'; while a third saw criminal women as 'hungry, poor, frustrated, powerless'.

Contrast these views with the considerably more buoyant and real-life experiences of some criminal women I interviewed. Mandy (cheque card fraud): 'It's quite a good game. It's the actress in me coming out.' Rebecca: 'The thing with me is – it is the money, but I also *like* doing it.' Jacki (conspiracy): 'To me it was all really a colourful adventure.' Although there is a grain of truth behind commonly held characterisations of criminal women, the insiders themselves generally have a much more resilient, and realistic, attitude towards their actions. Most crime committed by women is of an intensely practical, logical nature, carried out, 'ninety per cent of the time', as ex-prisoner Jenny Hicks stresses, 'because they cannot find an alternative way of making enough money'.

Any attempt at moral divisions between 'good' and 'bad' women – another popular diversion forged in the public imagination on the subject of crime – soon becomes futile when you talk to *any* women in depth about their daily lives. I asked several people – all *without* criminal records – whether they had ever broken the law. I have yet to find any woman, middle- and working-class alike, who has answered that question with a 'no'. Charlotte, a young, 'respectable', well educated white woman, casually admitted to each of the following, un-detected offences: shoplifting, theft, possession and smuggling of illegal drugs, and fraud! She also said, 'I would commit virtually any crime which got me money if I didn't think I'd get caught – as long as it didn't mean any physical harm to any other person, or if the person I was stealing from was poorer than me. I would commit any financial crime against the state if I didn't think I would get caught. I have stolen things from shops, public institutions, fiddled tube fares.... I don't feel guilty about these kinds of crimes.'

Shirley, a black woman in her mid-twenties, now (interestingly) working in the legal profession, remembers youthful bouts of stealing, and being a member of a shoplifting gang: 'It was exciting and thrilling. Although it wasn't so great being found out.' She also admits to more emotional urges to crime: 'I have wanted to murder some people because I've been at the end of my tether. But I would be too scared to do it.'

Fear of the consequences is the most powerful sanction against crime, for men and women. Women particularly, with their maternal conditioning, are inclined to hold back – even though their emotional frustration at restrictions on their lives may be huge. Margaret, a woman now in her sixties, remembers: 'Sadly, the crime of child battering comes about because of this frustration, I think. I had a long fuse as a mother, but now and again I was overcome by a consuming anger at the situation I found myself placed in, where I was the centre of several people's needs and immediate demands, and money was short. The intelligence needed to balance the money, the diets, the attention, and to share out what love I had between them all, nearly broke me several times. I knew if I once brought down my fist, I would not stop. So I never raised it. But it was a near thing every time.'

These few, sporadic, individual memories reveal how false is the divide we set up between 'criminal' and 'non-criminal' – how blurred the line between acceptable behaviour and censured action. The 'innocent' female paragon mentioned earlier is a damaging figment of society's imagination; as is the archetypal feminine victim. When talking about crime the most important thing to avoid – and yet the most often invoked reaction – is a pompous set of moral judgments. *None* of us is immune to the temptations of crime in some aspect or another. As Shirley says, 'Each and every one of us must have done something a bit naughty in our lives, and if we haven't, we really ought to have!'

WHAT IS CRIME?

Crime is a term used often, and glibly, to describe a whole range of censured behaviour, and yet, as writers Walsh and Poole admit in their *Dictionary of Criminology*, 'There is no word in the whole lexicon of legal and criminological terms which is so elusive of definition as the word "crime"...'[1] It is often used as a neat way of writing off 'undesirable' members of the community – the poor, the non-conformist, the rebellious – but when analysed properly, ceases to yield such comforting meanings.

Put simply, crime is a deliberate contravention of a country's laws, a punishable offence. Described in official jargon, crime is 'a concept whose necessary elements are proscribed action, evil intention, and prescribed punishment.... It fixes the definition of crime firmly in the person, and the intention of the diseased brain, as a moral sin, or as a subversive protest against the state.'

But there is an alternative view, which turns these official versions upside-down. Just as no woman should consider herself morally superior to another neither should the state itself, official arbiter on crime, believe itself above reproach. When people become moralistic about someone swindling their paltry Social Security payments, maybe they should think about this: Amelia, a black feminist and activist, believes that although 'crime is defined for us from early on as an offence against property, or person, or state, for me, crime is *violence* – violating a person's or a group's basic human rights, i.e. the right to live, to sleep, to eat. Therefore, I would define unemployment, for example, as a crime of the government against the people.'

Margaret, sixty, and still militant, sees crime in a broader sense, as violence: 'Simply, crime means violence, or destruction, or taking what is not yours. This includes – as well as all the obvious crimes – chopping down protected trees, tax evasion, polluting rivers.' These 'non-criminal' women I interviewed came up with such definitions unprompted; their view of crime easily expanded from the conventional 'crooks and muggers' imagery to include upper-class, or privileged, 'crooks': company directors involved in fraud; multinational companies destroying the environment. Their comments brought home how narrow the normal view of crime is, and how jaundiced we are in our perceptions of who – the male thug, the working classes, the poor and 'pathetic' woman, the powerless underdog – commits it.

Says Charlotte, 'There are two kinds of crime – things which are defined by law as crimes, and "moral" crimes. Crimes which are against the law can be split up into crimes against property and crimes against people. "Moral" crimes are things which I believe to be criminal, according to a more personal code which aims for fairness, equality and freedom for all people. In this category I would include things like war, making nuclear bombs, testing dubious contraceptives on women from the Third World, dumping polluting substances and forcing people to work in dangerous conditions because they are desperate for jobs.'

Many of these actions are not subject to legal restrictions. Why not? Charlotte again: 'In general the legal system is set up so that the kinds of crimes committed by poor people are punished with greater relative severity than crimes committed by rich powerful people. . . . The legal system functions only partly as a means of controlling anti-social behaviour and allowing people to live in peace. It is also a means by which powerful members of society control, repress and intimidate those who are *less* powerful, and maintain the social order in which they dominate.'

Juxtaposed with this are the politics of the 'less powerful', whose crime registers a protest, however oblique, at the regimes which *keep* them powerless. As one woman said: 'Robbing a rich department store when you are poor is a rebellion against the poverty imposed by capitalism.' Put more simply, as Shirley did, 'crime is an extreme form of communication' – communicating need, anger, hopelessness and self-defence.

Just like the myth of the 'innocent' and 'guilty' woman, pat pre-conceptions of what constitutes a crime all crumble when you look closely at the word, its misleading associations, its wider meanings, and the people who commit it.

WHAT IS A CRIMINAL?

Shake off the stereotypes, and you'll find that if the criminal offence is itself hard to define, the female offender behind it is even more elusive. Common images of the criminal are always male. Caroline, a well-informed colleague, nonetheless admitted that 'When I think of crime I think of men like the Krays and the Mafia. There is a male-dominated hierarchy in crime as elsewhere – no female "professionals".' There *are* female professionals, because I met some of them, but they are not given public recognition. Women criminals are already a threat – highly successful ones would be impossible to accept. So the criminal, if female, remains either a sad, victimised creature, or – usually – invisible.

If you want to be pedantic, then a criminal is someone who breaks the law of the land. However, as so many people have revealed to me, that is nearly every adult alive. Taking spare pens or paper from work places; paying less than full fare on buses; driving through red lights; taking more than your quota of booze or perfume through customs. . . . All these little naughtinesses add up. They do constitute a crime. And 'criminality', as one woman expressed it to me, 'is a relative concept which changes over time.' She went on, 'I don't believe in the concept of the "criminal". I don't believe that there are some people who are innately anti-social or evil.' Women who earn the label 'criminal', through repeated or big offences, are in no way a homogenous, easily defined group. They cut across class and colour (remembering that black and working-class women are more likely to be penalised, and often only have access to the less 'professional' and therefore more visible crimes, like shoplifting or prostitute-related offences). They also cut through old-fashioned perceptions of woman-hood like a knife. But read the mainstream literature on crime, and you really would not think so.

WHO IS THE WOMAN CRIMINAL? THE OFFICIAL VERDICT

There is a sweet, funny old rhyme I can remember my mother singing to me when I was a child: 'There was a little girl/And she had a little curl/Right in the middle of her forehead./And when she was good/She was very very good/But when she was bad, she was horrid'. Good girl; naughty girl. That idea, instilled from babyhood, of women being up there with the angels, or down below with the devil – picking apples like mad for a poor, unsuspecting Adam – is applied in an even less subtle way to female criminals. Somehow, as 'marked' women, they are easy meat for many crackpot male theories about the dangerous side of womanhood.

One fact cannot be disputed – women commit far less crime than men. Figures issued by the British Home Office for 1973 record 292,000 convictions of men for serious, 'indictable' offences, as opposed to only 45,200 similar convictions for women. Ten years on, in 1983, men were again up in the six-figure range – 398,400 – with women still only five figures, 62,700. The crimes women commit are usually not as serious as those committed by men, but their punishment is hardly less severe. Every so often a story breaks in the press about a woman being sent to prison for something as tiny as stealing a bottle of milk. How often do you hear similar stories about men? Women do less, but suffer more for it. The Women Prisoners' Resource Centre in London recorded that nearly *half* of the 3,000-odd female prison population in 1983 were there simply because they could not afford to pay their fines. They had not even been sentenced to prison in the first place. Most of their crimes, says the WPRC, were minor cases of stealing.

Criminology has treated women's role in crime with a large measure of indifference over the years. As in other areas of official history, women have been conspicuous mainly by their absence. But when they *are* discussed, a curious double-think sets in. Women have statistically proved themselves less violent, indeed less 'criminal' than men. NACRO – National Association for the Care and Resettlement of Offenders, the Home Office organisation – points out: from 293 violent women offenders arrested in 1977, only 68 were sentenced to more than twelve months imprisonment, 'suggesting that most women, even when convicted of violence, are not considered a serious threat to the public'.[2] Despite this fact, the theorists go more than a little 'hysterical' when approaching the female side of their subject matter. Writer Christine Rasche puts it succinctly when she says, 'The special problems of the delinquent woman have at all times been neglected – or glossed over by sentiment and unreliable male intuition'.[3]

From the nineteenth century onwards, criminology has suffered from the legacy of Lombroso and Ferrero (see chapter 4), biological determinists who saw female criminals as physical deviants – monstrous throwbacks to a more primitive era. Otto Pollak, writing in the 1920s, and later enjoying a renewed popularity in the 1960s, picked up on this warped notion when he implicated women not only as criminals in their own right, but as instigators of *male* crime too (a neat way of explaining away the embarrassing fact that men are far more criminally 'deviant' than women). How did he do this? Well, it all comes down to sex.... Women, he said, have the physiological ability to fake orgasms, while men's bodies cannot 'lie' during intercourse. In this way, women's bodies apparently make them 'natural' deceivers. Research done in the 1970s by Maggie Casburn showed that this sexual stereotyping starts early – with many young girls appearing in London courts, not for criminal offences, but for being perceived as 'morally in danger'. Whilst boys who ran away were referred to as 'a bit reckless' – tearaways – the girls were often connected with promiscuity, a very female 'offence.' This is similar to the classic misconception of prostitution as a search for love. W.I. Thomas, writing in the 1920s, made such an idea popular, despite persistent corrections by prostitutes themselves, who avow that 'preconceived notions that there'd be girls who'd do this for pleasure, are quite absurd...'[4]

Some of these ideas about criminal women seem to arise simply to make their originators feel better, to explain away blatant injustices (like incarcerating milk bottle stealers) and to avoid the awkwardness of confronting women who will not fit into neat little social boxes. Black and working-class women suffer the most discrimination in the courts and in the public's understanding of crime. According to the Black Female Prisoners' Scheme in Britain, although only 3 per cent of the population are black, an estimated 35 per cent of the female prison population are black. Margaret Valentine and Mavis Johnson, talking about prostitution in America, reckon that although the majority of women working the streets are white, 'prostitutes in prison are in the great majority black'.[5] Are we really to believe that black women are biologically or socially impelled to commit that much more crime? Hardly. Sue Shutter, talking about immigration law in Britain, told me of the grilling which black women have to go through should they wish to bring their husbands into the country (see chapter 2). As she says, 'That sort of thing gets a lot of women feeling like criminals, although obviously they're not.'

The same stereotyping happens to working-class women. Probation officer Andrea Duffy has noticed one particular class distinction: 'If a woman is middle-class, then people assume she does it because she's depressed. If the woman is working-class, then it's assumed to be an economic crime.' Black feminist Amelia challenged the assumptions Andrea Duffy describes, when I talked to her about crime. 'Those in power would believe a black woman or a working-class woman more ready to commit a crime than a white middle-class woman. I don't think this is necessarily true. I think middle-class and upper-class women commit crimes that are then hidden. But of course when black women and working-class women commit crimes, they do so out of necessity, and for good reasons – just as much as white women do.'

Periodically the media and the 'experts' start bleating about massive increases in crime. Since the 1970s the focus has shifted to include female as well as male offenders as the subject of these scares. Apex Trust, an organisation which finds work for ex-prisoners, records that 'crime figures for women have risen by 65 per cent between 1970 and 1981'. Along with all the old clichés about race and class, a new target for blame has hit the scene: women's liberation. Of all those women who refuse to fit into boxes, feminists are the most vocal in their defiance. As such, they are the most obvious source of fear and the most likely candidates for a smear campaign. Freda Adler started this off in a big way in the 1970s when she wrote, in *Sisters In Crime*, that 'technology and the women's liberation movement have equalised the capacity for male crimes, including violence'.[6] Women, she claimed, were becoming more like men in the pattern of their crime – an inflammatory suggestion, squashed on two counts by feminist criminologist Carol Smart. For a start, she says, tiny statistics are all too easily inflated into huge-sounding figures. Shock and horror over a '500 per cent' increase in murders by women between 1965 and 1975 is quickly deflated when you realise that the numbers involved have risen from just one to five! Secondly, the women's movement 'does not simply *cause* dissatisfactions, it is often the expression of *existing*. . .injustices and inequalities.'[7]

It is absurd to seek out scapegoats rather than confronting the reality behind the image. As Gillian Williams points out in her study of 'normal' and 'deviant' images of women: 'If a woman does not behave "normally", then questions are asked about her hormones or her "poor relations" with her father, not whether there is something wrong with the identikit picture of the normal woman.'[8]

It's time the identikit was dismantled and a newer, more realistic version built up. If we look at women's own experiences of crime, rather than the false images constructed around them, then the 'monsters' disappear. The female criminal ceases to be 'one of them', and comes nearer to being just 'one of us'.

CRIMINAL WOMEN: THE REALITY

The only way you can ever learn why women commit crime – a rare and bold act in a society which expects its female members to be nothing but exemplary – is to talk to those who have done it. The women I interviewed are very different individuals – in age, class, race and background – and they fit into no conventional pigeonholes. But certain key words and recurring themes emerged from their conversation – five factors which go some way towards an explanation of their criminal involvement. Why do they do it? For money; from anger; for success; for kicks – and out of pure need. Let them tell their own stories. . . .

For money

Beat up little seagull on a marble stair
Tryin' to find the ocean, lookin' everywhere

Hard times in the city, in a hard town by the sea
Ain't nowhere to run to
There ain't nothin' here for free...

('Baltimore' by Randy Newman, *Baltimore* album, Nina Simone,
CTI Records)

The main reason why most women commit crime is quite simple: it's for money. As Jenny Hicks has pointed out, a woman often cannot find a legitimate way of earning enough cash to survive. The chances are she will be unemployed, or low down in the wages market; and she will often have children and/or a partner to support. Only 10 per cent of female crime, says Jenny, has anything to do with violence. Ninety per cent is theft of property, and 60 per cent of this is for stuff worth less than £100. And when you realise that it costs £363 to keep a woman in prison for just a week in Britain (1983 Prison Department figures), the punishment hardly seems to fit the crime.

As the gap between consumer temptations and actual earning power gets greater in the Western world, a pent-up sense of frustration grows with it. Crime writer Lynda La Plante says of television – a key target for advertisers and high tech soap operas: 'That bloody box is such an incentive to crime, and such an incentive to severe hopelessness. It must be the most awful, horrific thing when you have a husband unemployed, a kid on drugs, you've got no money, you're living in a shithouse, and you turn on, and there's *Dallas*...' In every big city in Britain there are huge numbers of unemployed people, and more and more people begging for money on the streets. But just as evident are the glossy hoardings advertising expensive drinks, exotic holidays, exclusive clothes. The irony of such a contradiction is a violent one and can understandably lead to extreme reactions: to crime.

Poverty is indeed a primary motive for many women's crimes. Mandy first got into stealing and cheque card fraud when she lost her job through looking after her sick child. But throughout this period her sense of morality was strong – a striking factor of many women's offending: 'I'd never steal from individuals, only rip off banks and shops.' She even extended this pattern into a neigh-bourly support network: 'I'd be thieving for six families (on the housing estate) – just like Robin Hood. I know a lot of people who do that.'

Maria, meanwhile, was taking food from supermarkets (with consummate skill) in her teens, in order to feed the girls in the flat where she was staying. Unable to pay rent, she could at least provide an evening meal. She got so good at it that leg of lamb became a regular feature on the menu. (Once she did get caught, 'meat-handed', by a policeman. 'What's your address then?' 'Ain't got one.' 'Oh, gonna eat that lamb raw were you?' 'Yeah, that's right...') But there were times when she was so poor and hungry – after repeated lockups in police cells – that she had to beg chocolate from people in the street. Eventually she lost her nerve for stealing altogether: 'I don't do it now. I can't even nick a bubblegum now.' Mandy also has stopped stealing, because she has since married, her husband is straight, and he doesn't like her doing it – a neat reversal of traditional stereotypes!

For Rebecca, the desire for money and a genuine excitement at 'kiting' (cheque card fraud) go side by side: 'I just get a kick out of it. I mean I like the money. I like being able to say to my kids, "Yeah, sure you can have a tenner to go out and get a new toy." We grew up with nothing – I like them to have whatever they want.' Money can be a passport to a better life, a means of gaining dignity and self-respect, as well as giving access to useful goods. It can buy you – superficially at least – out of your class.

Since a woman's livelihood is traditionally bound up with her body – with financial dependence first on father, and then on husband – it's unsurprising that selling her body in a more blatant financial transaction – one *not* illegal, but nonetheless often criminalised – features largely throughout history. The English Collective of Prostitutes: 'One way women had always found to get financial independence, or any finances at all, was pro-stitution.'[9] As the ECP bluntly conclude, only when money is freely available to woman will the 'oldest profession in the world' die out – 'the end of poverty is the end of prostitution.'[10]

People have constructed elaborate, sexy theories about why

women become prostitutes, theories which probably fuel their powers of fantasy rather than reflecting the harsh reality. Thus Cecil Bishop can wax moral and lyrical: 'No doubt many people will be shocked to learn that most prostitutes deliberately choose prostitution as their occupation.... She finds that prostitution affords an easy if comparatively small income, and that it satisfies a sex craving which grows in proportion to the extent that it is indulged.'[11] But there is no intimacy, and rare enjoyment for the prostitute. On one thing only is Bishop right: the money. As one prostitute says, 'There's no mystery – if it weren't for the money then I'd rather be doing any other job than this one.'[12]

Rebecca, although born into a criminal environment, where family and friends are often involved in major crimes, also needs and wants a 'proper' job, seeking her due respect: 'Now I've always been a worker, and I still always *do* work if I can.' But the clothes she and her family wear are Italian, expensive, exclusive: fruits of illegal, as well as legal, work. Money, which is used as the passport to respect by business and professional people the Western world over, is accurately perceived by 'criminal women' as one of their only means to survival. If they must break some laws to survive (often not made with their interests at heart in the first place), then break them they do.

From anger

> Last night, I felt like
> Smashing my head in a clear glass window,
> But instead, I went out
> And smashed up the phone booth round the corner...
>
> ('I felt like smashing my face', Yoko Ono, Bootleg tape)

A lot of the women here aren't used to talking about their feelings at great length, and they do tend to react to things with action. Many of their crimes have constituted a reaction because they're angry at something. They see they're getting back at the system by committing crimes, rather than acting out the middle-class view, which is that they're actually victims of the system. They see that they're *rebels*.

(Janet Urry, worker at a hostel for women ex-prisoners in London)

No-one expects a woman to be openly angry; it is seen as a fearful break with her femininity if she is – hence people's greater shock at the stroppy female drunk, than at a blaspheming, boozed-up bloke. That same anger, a sense of breaking loose, is never thought of as a primary cause for women's crime, even though the rebellious, window-smashing male is a commonplace stereotype. Women are expected to turn their anger inwards, to smash up their *own* faces. But they do not always comply. Much women's crime is inspired by frustrated fury – maybe disguised and muted more than with the men, but fury, just the same. No, a woman's anger does not always express itself in loud words and wild fighting, but when it comes, it can have shocking repercussions:

> *Prison doctor*: 'I do not really feel she is a murderer. If you look into her face, her eyes, you will never believe that so gentle a woman can commit murder.'
> *Dr Saadawi*: 'Who says murder does not require that a person be gentle?'[13]

This startling excerpt comes from the true story of a Middle Eastern woman called Firdaus, who was forced into prostitution from an early age, and who finally went to her death on charges of murder. The man she killed was her pimp.

When the author, Nawal El Saadawi, visited her in prison, she elicited the baffled statement above from an uncomprehending prison doctor. What Firdaus did was escape from an unbearable situation, where she had been abused for years. Now she was fighting back. This doctor was judging her action according to her supposed 'femininity', instead of looking at all the underlying and understandable causes of her action. He was denying her, as a woman, a certain freedom of will. This is not to say also 'a freedom to *kill*', but an awareness, lacking in most modern societies, that women too have their limits, that their motherly patience is not inexhaustible, that they do have spirits of resistance and a means to rebel against untenable situations. They have got tempers too – and they are not to be dismissed as 'hysterics'. The anger is real.

As Janet Urry also explained, 'the violent crimes have been very much to do with personal situations': lovers, husbands, relations, who have carried these women to the end of their tether. Jayne, a woman in her thirties to whom I talked, had killed her husband. She went down for several years, and found inevitable problems on her release: 'When you come out you are expected to show sorrow, penitence, remorse. But you may have done it out of *anger*. And when people ask you why, you want to say, "because he bloody well deserved it". It's the one thing you're not allowed to say.'

Time after time I had to confront my own prejudices when I talked to women charged with violent offences. Often I didn't know what women had done before visiting them – in prison or at home – each time what they said was a shock. 'Such a calm person, such a kind person, such a polite person – how could she do *that*?' Each time thoughts like those of Saadawi's prison doctor would run through my head, and I had to readjust my mind to let their own reasons come through to me. One thing is certain: stereotypes of rabid, wild-eyed murderesses are dangerously far from the truth. When I talked to women who had killed, I usually had a sense that they had an awesome understanding of what had happened. They knew the reasons for their action, the consequences, and the meaning. Each had acted from a deep emotional volition.

But sometimes things backfire. Anger, its lid on so tightly for women, can sometimes explode and hit the wrong target. Maria, a young woman with a history of some violence and 'psychiatric disturbance', gives one example of just busting loose: 'I attacked this girl and just charged her like a rugby tackle, and I had her splattered all over the pavement. It wasn't even her that I was angry at. It was something that had happened, and I just took it out on her. Her teeth were like piano keys ... I felt terrible then. I felt really bad, man. I've never felt so bad in all my life.'

After the anger comes guilt, and frustration at her wasted energy: 'I want normal things. I want a flat. I want a job, a car. People of my age have usually got them. I've got sweet fuck all.'

Often women's crime expresses a fury at glaring social injustice. As Janet Urry explained, 'Shoplifting crimes are done because, "Well, I'm entitled to it. I haven't any money."' Mandy, who has worked at shoplifting and cheque card frauds talks of the morality in the anger of her actions: 'There were times when I was younger, when I'd see a dress, not worth very much, costing £25, and I'd steal it rather than pay. The people who charge that amount are thieves already.'

Rebecca, a 'kiter', has a similar sense of morals, a revulsion at injustice. She can rip the banks off for thousands of pounds, yet expresses genuine grief and incomprehension at an incident on her own housing estate, where a home help stole £300 from an old lady: 'Now that's something I would never do. I found £10 at work the other day and put it on top of the locker in case it belonged to anyone. That kind of crime that people do (taking from someone infirm or poor) just turns me over. I can't understand why people wanna be like that.'

The idea that women's criminal reactions are just an 'intuitive mystery' is no more true for them than for men. In fact, as Steph Blackwell, a former worker with Apex Trust replied, when I asked if the women offenders who she saw had been 'irrational'. 'No', she said, 'it was much more the case that the *men* were totally bloody irrational. A few pints too many – a beer glass in the face, and then they were up before the courts.'

Genuine feelings of anger and mutiny in women, because they are not allowed free rein, can sometimes appear like a defensive mask, rather than real anarchy. So crime, or activities associated with crime, like prostitution, can be a formalised way in which women can escape from their other stereotype: the submissive and socially sanctioned one. It is not always exactly a release, but a means of self-protection, and can become a 'vulgar' caricature in itself. Says one prostitute: 'I've got a sort of split personality. In the daytime, I'm myself, I do my shopping, live like any other woman; and at night I'm a real prostitute, with the slang, the vulgarity, the behaviour, the violence and the rebellion, the temper. And all this, apart from the rebellion I've always been into, isn't in my nature. Vulgarity is like make up, it's a defence mechanism, a sort of protective second skin.'[14]

It is impossible to escape male/female role-playing in a society which sets such store by strict sexual divisions. Since anger is assumed to be far more 'natural' for the man, women who get involved in crime often assume the angry petulance of a *male* criminal – to express an otherwise inexpressible rebellion. As one social worker explained, from her work with ex-prisoners, 'A lot of the women who commit crime will model themselves on men ... If it's burglary or violence, quite often they will come across as being quite macho.' Even the female rebel is too easily made into the masculinised 'freak'.

All this anger is not, of course, confined to women who commit crime. The seeds are there in us all. A famous woman crime writer told me of her own recent outburst. She owns a sportscar, a luxury she has worked for, and waited to have. As she parked it one day, a young punk walked past, spat at the car and hissed 'fucking cunt'. The owner, far from shrinking away, leapt up to her, seized her by the shoulders and screamed: 'What did you call me? How do you think I earned this car? Do you think I'm a "tart"? Suddenly you could see the fear in her eyes. I wouldn't let her go. I was just as violent as she was.' Her reaction was an understandable one, in the face of un-reasonable provocation, and would not have seemed at all out of place if a man were doing it – but it was shocking to hear it come from a woman, even to the ears of another woman, someone herself dressed in the (punk) uniform of defiance and fury. Drawing wider con-clusions, the sports car owner and writer was frighteningly philo-sophical: 'I think woman is much deeper, more controlled [than man] through generations of being suppressed. If you release that control ... then out comes the violence...'

For success

Crime as recognition and creative success in itself? Well, the great train robber Ronald Biggs managed it – even ended up in films. He is a big daddy hero now, and there's plenty more where he came from. So what about women? Traditionally, success for women has meant husband and family. Now it has come to mean career *and* family. On the surface, Western society has accepted the idea of public success for its women. But in reality it is a hard road, riddled with harassment and blocked by the closed doors of 'jobs for the boys'. Many of the women I spoke to wanted a success which was often only available – by reason of class and gender – by 'illegitimate' means.

Although some of these stories really are in one sense 'success stories' – of a job well done, and crime achieved by breathtaking artistry – always the conflict imposed by gender lurks under the surface. As Diana Christina wrote in her complex account of a life in crime, in *Criminal Women*,[15] although she always enjoyed the adrenalin of being a professional criminal, she could never reconcile that side of her life with being a loving mother – her dual qualities of 'healing hands, stealing hands' clashed and never complemented each other. Such a split is not as big an issue for criminal men, often supported as they are by wives and families: wives who, as Rebecca told me from her own experience, often bear the brunt of police harassment, yet remain remarkably loyal and steadfast to their spouses.

It is hard not to admire some of the exploits successful criminal women pull off. Steph Blackwell, of Apex Trust, told me about a client she met, an unexpected person on the criminal circuit: 'One woman I got to know was a fraud case. She was a real "mumsy" type, in her forties, lived in Brighton with her mother, worked in a bank and was *terribly* respectable. It turned out that she had been milking the bank for ten years for an enormous amount of money. She said in court that she didn't see why she and her mother shouldn't have all the good things in life ... She also said she was *so* surprised that it had taken all these men *such* a long time to find her out! She was unrepentant, was sent down for 18 months, starting off in Holloway but then transferred to an open prison, because she was so quiet and well-behaved.'

There's no doubt – it *can* work in a woman's favour, the prejudice which says females can't possibly do something so naughty (or so clever?). But that's often only if the accent is right too...

Jenny Hicks is another case of successful fraud: £¾ million

extracted from the post office by fiddling the business franking machine over a period of ten years. For her, crime was not a rebellion against the norm, but, ironically, a way of being *accepted*, of earning respect, and surmounting the limited opportunities imposed on her by a working-class background. She told me: 'I'd obviously rebelled against the norm for women, and I was seeking alternative ways of achieving an identity, but *within* the traditional system, because I wasn't the kid who broke the rules. I was very much the conservative kid who kept all the rules and upheld the traditions. But I wanted success, and I found emotional success very difficult to achieve, and therefore I'd gone into business to achieve *material* success, which is one way for a woman on her own to achieve some kind of status.'

She started her own business with a male partner and they later began operating a fraud system within their own company. She talks of the criminal nature of even 'respectable' businesses: 'When you're in business to make the maximum amount of profit, you have to play by all the rules that everyone else is playing, because of the competition.... The *accepted* frauds are your tax returns – claiming for certain expenses you didn't have ... To make money in a capitalist world you have to make it off the backs of other people. That is itself a crime – and one which definitely had its effects on me.'

She followed the normal capitalist practices: employing women at cheaper rates, offering low job security, planning the lowest possible outlay for the highest possible returns – in short, being a sharp business woman. As she says: 'After the ripping off of the people, the ripping off of the post office didn't seem that difficult, or that wrong.'

But the business retained 'a very respectable front. We worked for charities and for well-established companies.' This was white collar crime, and for that, 'You don't run with the other criminals – you're a respectable businesswoman.'

Later, bored with her undoubted success, Jenny *did* start to 'run with the criminals'. She took risks, and got involved in a dicey directory fraud, which led to her post office fraud being discovered – landing her in jail for five years. Later still she became politicised – whilst in prison – and co-founded a theatre group, the widely-acclaimed Clean Break Theatre, which became a different outlet for her creativity.

But she remains clear and unrepentant on what involved her in crime in the first place: 'It was knowing that you cannot make it on the accepted level, knowing that you want to be equal, don't want to rely on a man to provide wealth, but you still want that wealth. Now, the alternatives available are very limited. You can turn directly to crime or you can try and make it as a career woman – and without the kind of background for that, it's difficult.'

Twenty-five years ago, when Jenny was starting out on adult life, a profession for someone of her background was out: 'University had been wiped out for me by the teachers' expectations of what I should have.' The only option left to an ambitious, intelligent woman, was – business. 'Business in the end turned out to be synonymous with crime anyway.'

A luxurious lifestyle ensued. She bought her mum a house. 'I was able to charter a plane to go and see the monster in Loch Ness...' She flitted from hotel to hotel in Paris and Amsterdam, cushioned always from the real world, safe in her success – but bored, and corrupted. The experience has given her political insight: 'I found being a woman in business was definitely very tough, much tougher than for my partner. People naturally refer to the male as the boss... I had to be twice as strong, twice as rigid.

'Although what Maggie Thatcher has been doing is wicked, I do in a way understand it... I think she must go through the same things I did – that she's got to be that much more rigid, otherwise she's gonna lose control.'

For all its profoundly negative aspects, Jenny's experience of crime – now transcended by work in theatre – gave her what she initially sought in life: ten years of material success.

Rebecca described the same need for the high life, the same daring pride in her criminal activities. When she practised cheque card fraud, it was not just the ordinary banks, but the top class ones: 'You've got to have a lot of money before you even start off with them; I used to take my minder – pretend he was my chauffeur, and hand my parcels over to him.'

Does she not get scared at the risk involved in flying so high? 'I think the first one you lay down after a period of time (is scarey). But what happens is, you come to think of it as yours. It's your money. It isn't anybody else's. You *are* that name... (on the cheque card).'

What it takes, she says, is panache: 'You've got to be confident. You can't be stiff. I mean I've done it paralytic drunk. I've even gone in the same supermarket three times [in a day]... You know the store detectives and you know the security guards and you also know the security guards aren't looking for you kiting [they're looking for shoplifters]. You suss it out.'

Professionalism does not always match up to the need for recognition. One woman I spoke to, who mixes in criminal circles, talks of some 'flashy' characters with their fox furs and jewellery: 'These women, with their clothes and that, they wanna say, "Look, I'm not just your little slut. I can do things too." They're the ones who do it and get nicked.' There is a need, she continues, for caution and care – especially now, with the new hologram cheque cards (from which the signatures cannot be cleaned, and so have to be traced and copied). 'Some girls think it's so easy. And now of course it's an automatic five years. The banks have lost so much money.'

But the rewards of criminal success are greater, for her, than the risks: 'I can go out and in an hour I can earn two thousand. It's gotta far outweigh the fear of getting nicked.'

Crime has often been linked with frustrated energy and creativity, and there are a number of ex-prisoners who have successfully turned to art, literature and theatre. As Jenny Hicks says, many women possess a deep need for self-expression: 'Crime seems one way of getting rid of that energy.' Conversely, she says, 'you need energy and inventiveness for crime.' Other women interviewed echo her sentiments. Mandy, quoted at the start of the chapter, mentioned an artist's delight in her ability to steal and cheat. Jacki Holborough, co-founder of ex-prisoners' theatre group Clean Break with Jenny Hicks (see chapter 2), described the joy of seeing that artistry used in positive expressions of creativity. When she first started working with women at Askham Grange prison on theatrical productions, she says: 'I thought "God, they've got all this potential, all this talent – and what's being done to foster it? Nothing. If we weren't having this workshop now, they'd just be knitting in corners."'

Within a society which still secretly longs for women to just sit and knit, is it any wonder some of them find their only legitimate

of creative ability through unsanctioned and illegitimate
...s one woman who works with ex-prisoners explained: 'It's
...nding a better life really. And it isn't always a better life to go
...it.'

For kicks

> Jesus died for somebody's sins – but not mine...
>
> People say beware
> But I don't care
> The words are just rules and regulations to me.

('Gloria', Patti Smith, *Horses* Album, Arista)

There is a monstrous relic left over in western minds from the time
of Eve and the birth of Christianity – a voice which says 'Thou
shalt not have fun. And if thou hast fun, and if thou art a *woman* and
hast fun – by god, thou shalt pay for it.' So the idea that women
can commit crime, get away with it, *and* do it for enjoyment, is
probably the most controversial and unpalatable idea of all. It's
fine for men to be rebels – witness the 'cheerful cockney criminal'
types of the British television series *Minder* and *Porridge*, and the
endless 'sexy' stories of bad boys like Ronald Biggs, the Kray
Brothers, and Norman Mailer's romantic entanglement with
Death Row murderers in the States. For women rebelliousness is
not acceptable. This was highlighted at a recent Clean Break
performance in London, when a woman in the audience
commented: 'There are women who shoplift because they haven't
got any money ... and women who shoplift for kicks: and I think
the latter should take stock of themselves – get involved with
community work, or charities.' There it is again – knitting-in-
corners syndrome. But some women will not comply. Out of all
the complex reasons for crime which I discussed with hostel
worker Janet Urry, she also acknowledged the simple act of
rebellion; 'Sometimes – it's just for a laugh.'

Mandy, having turned to cheque card fraud initially for money reasons, nonetheless admits to feeling a thrill at the audacity of her actions: 'You get a real buzz out of it, pitting your wits against the banks and the post office. You come out of one morning's work and you've done a grand. . . .' Both she and another woman who was briefly involved in 'kiting', talked of the 'adrenalin pumping' as they moved in on the banks. As Mandy said, it was so much better being 'up front' than waiting in the car (an accomplice role often allotted to the women).

This adrenalin high led Mandy into work abroad within organised crime syndicates: 'You did it for the excitement. It was the first time I'd been abroad, and we stayed in posh hotels and ate and drank well . . . it was a real buzz – going through to Geneva, across the Alps, by cab.'

There is a widespread misconception – dating back to the 'biological passivity' theories of Lombroso and beyond – which assumes that women are either totally good or totally crackers. Probation officer Andrea Duffy, who has worked in a women's bail hostel and a male probation hostel, was given the same line: 'I kept being told that women were much more "difficult" than men. But the women had more character. Men are like sheep.'

Adolescent girls often show the same – sometimes unnerving – high spirits. And when those spirits are contained, they can turn to aggression. Steph Blackwell says that the most frightening place she ever visited as an employment worker for Apex Trust, was Bullwood Hall, a youth custody centre which is crammed with the exuberant energy of young women cooped up. Boys are not the only ones who need to climb trees and run a bit wild – and they are not the only ones to react when that freedom is denied them. When Steph Blackwell walked into Bullwood with her recently broken arm in a sling, she could feel the incredible tension – and the pairs of eyes watching from high above the courtyard. ''Ere!' shouted a disembodied voice, unidentifiable and invisible. 'Come up 'ere and I'll break the other one for you. . .' Her offer was not taken up.

The same high-pitched adrenalin drives older women too, when they go off on thieving sprees. Says Maria: 'I could go up to people selling jewellery on the street, grab a handful of silver chains and they'd be WHOOP! – down my sleeve – before they could even blink.

'I got a kick out of it. I loved doing it. I used to go out with a big baggy pair of jeans on, about ten sizes too big, and I'd go into the changing room, put on about three pairs of strides, then put my baggy pants back on and walk out, all stiff legged. . . I had a lot of bottle, a lot of nerve.'

Maria's early criminal life showed a recklessness which would later turn sour, and get her involved in psychiatric treatment. But she tells some gleeful stories of her less painful exploits: 'I've been done for fraud. I tried to get money out of a post office account that wasn't mine. My signature was crap. One thing I'm not good at is forgery. He took one look at it and pressed this button and the doors had locked. I was gonna go through the glass, but the kids had just come out of school and there were about 15 of them outside, trying to get in the shop. So I'm frantic, trying to get out of this bloody place – but I couldn't have dived through that window. . . I would have done if it hadn't been for the kids.'

Jenny Hicks talks of similar rebellious feelings when, bored with her business career, she got involved in a dodgy directory fraud, sending out fake invoices for non-existent advertising. 'I found this exciting,' she says. While her earlier business venture, swindling the post office on the side, was a quest for success, '*This* was an act of rebellion'. The man who had asked her to join his racket was carelessly casual about the crime: 'It was his cavalier attitude that somehow picked out in me a need to break free – so I went for it.'

Romantic adventure was the lure for Jacki Holborough's innocent involvement in complicated conspiracy charges – which first started with a troubleshooting investigation of illicit diamond leaks in South Africa, and ended with her charged (wrongly) with several others of demanding money with menaces, and conspiracy to assault. Throughout her complicated, incredible story, she repeatedly told me that it had all been 'above my head in many ways', and that she had become entangled through a genuine belief of the basic legitimacy of the whole 'adventure' (into which she was introduced by a friend) and for the thrill of overseas travel, and the colourful figures she met.

The troubleshooter who started the whole thing going had first asked Jacki to put dramatic adverts for helpers in London magazines: 'You will be involved in journalistic coverage, investigating, fisticuffs. . .' Such is the stuff of James Bond movies – and it landed Jacki (later to be co-founder of Clean Break – and herself an actress) with a three-year jail sentence. The price of adventure is high.

Out of need

When I talked to Chris Tchaikovsky of Women In Prison about this book, she emphasised one thing about women and crime. 'Please,' she said, 'don't glamorise it.' There *are* exotic aspects, and funny stories; there are political activists, like the Greenham women, and rebels who survive the system. But, she says, the majority of female prisoners are 'very poor, disadvantaged women, who are not very articulate, who can't read very well. . .' Ignored, unhappy people. Often women's crime is glibly connected with psychiatric disturbance (discussed in chapter 4), but this section steers clear of that emotive argument, while still recognising instances of desperate measures, taken in situations of great need.

Pat Carlen, in her 1983 study of a Scottish women's prison, says, of the people she spoke to, 'They could not be romanticised (I did not interview any female Jimmy Boyles!), their series of short-term sentences could not easily be turned into odysseys of psychological survival.'[16] These women, like many of those in prisons throughout Britain, were there for small-time offences related to shoplifting and petty theft. The crime women commit is often one of impoverished, unheeded desperation.

A senior probation officer from the North of England, Mr A., said, when I asked him which crimes the women he had seen over the years were mostly involved in: 'Domestic crimes (meter fiddling, social security fraud) committed by women under financial pressure, for example, one-parent family mother living on social security benefits and struggling to make ends meet. . . The offences are often a response to a crisis.'

Often, he added, these women take the responsibility for small crimes committed by husbands or male lovers because the men have a criminal record, and would go down for a longer period. Crime, he maintains, is still predominantly a male preserve: 'Generalising, it seems to me that males initiate criminal behaviour and the wives/girl-friends seem to play a subordinate role.'

Sometimes, however, the spotlight turns to the women themselves. When this happens, it can be a revolt against those very men they supported for so long.

Jayne, in prison herself for killing a husband she could no longer endure, told me of one terrible case where a woman had starved her baby to death. It took four months for the baby to die, during which time it was even eating its own excrement. How could anyone do such a thing? Seen in cool objectivity it seems indefensible. But as Jane said, this woman's husband had walked out on her. She identified the baby with her wrecked marriage, her ruined life. She simply closed off from the world – ceased to care for her baby, ceased to care for herself.

On a less horrifying level, Maria, with a history of theft behind her, told me, 'The rest of my stuff has been criminal damage – just a way of getting back inside because I've had nowhere to go.'

Poverty and homelessness – and rarely the right person there at the right time to take care of her – led Maria to acts of minor desperation: 'Putting bottles through police station windows, things like that.' All to get herself arrested, and have somewhere to stay for the night – if only a police cell. When she was 17, and first went down, she says, 'I didn't even want to come out of prison. I loved it there.'

Maria's stormy adolescence catapulted her into an adulthood of aggression and desperation, leading to stays in psychiatric hospitals (see chapter 4). Her description of events leading up to this show how little she was integrated into any 'normal' social structure, and how needy she was – a need nobody was fully capable of answering.

She had been over to Amsterdam, and while there, she had been arrested for begging: 'I asked Old Bill for a guilder for a bag of chips and he nicked me.'

After a week in a Dutch jail, she was sent home, weak with flu –

compounding her illness with drugs handed to her on a London street. Crazed with tiredness, and tripping badly, she knew only one way of finding help – getting arrested again: 'I thought "I've gotta get wicked" so I got a stone and threw it at a sign. Then I put a bottle through the police station window, and about 15 policemen came rushing out. I got a whack on the nose from the sergeant. There was blood pouring out of me snick, and then I got some nice attention from a policewoman who dabbed it better... That was all I needed, something like that. When you're young you need that sort of thing don't you?'

There is a mixture of humour and pathos in her story – and a good deal of awareness: 'I've got nothing against Margaret (Thatcher) but ever since she was in power, I've not been able to get a job.'

Before 1979, when the radical right shifted the pattern of employment so drastically, Maria would do the rounds of building sites, picking up casual work easily – she's strong and dextrous. But now even the lowly-rated manual jobs are few and far between, so there is little chance for Maria to keep her troubled life stable by being employed. Hostels and trust schemes do their best to help such women as Maria, but government back-up is scant – and money and jobs cannot be created from thin air. Also, women are always the first to go from the labour market, as low-skilled and undervalued workers.

Annette's crime was precipitated by an emotional overburden. She started a small fire in the place where she was working. Her job as nurse there was impossibly demanding – she has since been replaced by *four* people, doing the same job! – and she snapped under pressure: 'The only thing I knew was, I *had* to get out of that building.'

Her action was not particularly devastating since she knew the sophisticated alarm system would pick up the fire signal within minutes – which it did – and would thereby provide her with a rational means of 'escape'. Her story is told at greater length in chapter 4, and charts a troubled history in family and adult life, which she has struggled, with a phenomenal strength of will, to resolve. Her arson was perhaps one way of communicating that there was something badly wrong with her life.

The strain of being female – of having to fulfil complex contradictory roles: worker, lover, mother, wife; or twist yourself inside out to *escape* them – is undoubtedly a factor in some women's crime. But this is not to blame it on female biology. Richard Ford, ex-warden of Britain's only all-female bail hostel, draws a useful distinction between biology and conditioning: 'Crime is not necessarily to do with a woman's biology, but it is very clearly to do with a woman's *role*. A woman in her late 30s, a first offender, someone who has not fallen into the acceptable ways for a woman – no child or husband etc. – may feel a large psychological burden from society, which could account for her crime.'

Expectations for women to be all things at once, in an era which equates emancipation with being superwoman, bring strains on some women in their forties, feels crime writer Lynda La Plante: 'They feel that they should do things – and they can't. They're not all ready for it.' So social *demands*, as well as social deprivation, can lead to feelings of inadequacy, can push someone – often unintentionally – into crime.

Anne describes her drug addiction, which started with the failure of her marriage, and ended with drug-induced violence, and prison:

'I was just past 18 and my marriage broke up. I was hanging around with a group of friends and got into smack straight off, and it just led from there till I was an addict.

'I was going out with this young guy at the time – he was quite straight – and his parents and my parents wanted us to marry, but I was just getting worse and worse. I started getting eight fixes a day. I don't know why... I suppose I felt a failure.

'This young guy I was going out with, he wanted to get married... but I just could not get off it by then. I might have loved him, I don't know. You don't think of things like that when you're a junky. You've got no emotions whatsoever. One night he'd drunk about eight pints of Special Brew plus amphetamines.' He was in a state, and so was she: 'I'd had a fix but I'd missed, so my arm was all swollen up. I hadn't had a hit so I'd drunk a load as well. He just started rowing, saying I was getting involved with someone else and all this. I told him to shut up. I was cutting sandwiches up and he started waving a knife at me. So I grabbed the knife and I stabbed him with it. I barely remember it – I didn't do it seriously – I just grabbed the knife, I was so annoyed with him. By then he'd wound me up so much. I just went like that to him (imitates lunging motion) and first time it went straight into his heart. He fell over, and I thought he was mucking about – thought he was drunk; and I was slapping his face. But then I realised, when I saw the blood all over the kitchen floor. I called an ambulance, we went to the hospital and a nurse came out half an hour later and told me he was dead.'

When Anne was arrested and sent to prison, all sorts of psychiatric tests were made on her (see chapter 4) to try to prove her mental disturbance. She remained obstinate – blamed it on the drugs: 'Anyone with that amount of gear (heroin) in them, and that amount of drink, would obviously turn into a flippin' psychopath' – and managed, in her months inside, to work out for herself the guilt, fear, horror and depression brought on by the violence into which she had been plunged.

There is a tendency to blame women for all kinds of misery, when they are often the sufferers, not the perpetrators. Obvious targets for this moralism are prostitutes. But their culpability is open to debate. Probation officer Mr A. talks of the soliciting and theft which is often initiated by men: 'My experience is that prostitution and crime run hand-in-hand, and that the male associates of prostitutes tend to have criminal records so that the girls are often encouraged to commit offences.'

C. in *Prostitutes: Our Life* looks at the deeper issue: 'Some people say we exploit the sexual misery created by this society. In a way it's true, but it's not us who create the sexual misery, and I think we're more its victims than its exploiters.'[17]

Sharon Pollock has written a play called *Blood Relations*, about Lizzie Borden, who, in 1892, was accused of killing her father and her stepmother with an axe. In the play, Pollock ascribes 'motive' to the fact that her parents are conspiring to have her inheritance stopped (her only means of survival) since she does not intend to marry. As a son she would automatically get the money. As a daughter, she must marry, otherwise she will quite literally be starved into submission.

Just as interesting as the play itself is Sharon Pollock's explanation of why she wrote it: 'Prior to working in the theatre I was married for some years to a violent man. I spent a great deal of time devising, quite literally, murderous schemes to rid me of him...

'I would not have killed to prevent injury to myself... I would have killed to maintain my sense of self, to prevent a violation that was far more frightening and threatening than any blow, and of which physical violence against my person was the only outward manifestation. And so it is with Lizzie.'[18]

Whatever differences and difficulties men may have through class, race, circumstances, their physical and emotional independence is still their birthright. For a woman, despite vast and continuing social changes, autonomy of action is still something for which she must fight. Female crime can be an expression of that struggle: a deep-rooted need to be free, sometimes articulated, sometimes not, set against an intransigent system of values which blocks this bid for freedom. However petty or massive the crime there is an expression of her *self* – either tortured, defiant, or just plain impoverished – which is inveitably caught up inside her action. As Rebecca says, 'All (criminal) women wanna say is, "Look, shit, hold on, slow down – I'm here, and I *matter*".'

PAYING FOR
IT: POLICE,
THE LAW,
THE COURTS

'I naively believed if you were guilty you were found guilty, if you were innocent you were found innocent.... There were two people in the dock with myself and Michael, whom I *knew* to be innocent – but they were found guilty. That was a tremendous shock to me.' (Jenny)

'...anyone who trusts a woman is trusting thieves.' (Hesiod, eighth-century Greek philosopher)

'You can't win. At the end of the day you're the victim.' (Marianne)

'The law, solely and expressly, is there for the exploitation of those who do not understand it.' (Bertolt Brecht, *Threepenny Opera*)

Despite the bold defiance of the law which motivates some women to commit crime, as chapter 1 describes, the odds are invariably stacked against them. Even a petty crime committed by a woman is a huge revolt against male authority and expected female behaviour – and is punished accordingly. The law does not like 'deviant' women. Historically, after all, a woman has always been expected to serve her man: first father, then husband. Always dependent and subordinate, women have rarely been given much status in law, other than that of passive vessel. Henry VIII's Statute of Wills set the pattern for centuries to come when it lumped together 'married women, infants, and mental incompetents' and debarred them from making wills – or indeed, from making laws. The ancient lawmakers never even considered that women, like men, might *break* these lofty statutes! Even the timeless laws of custom which the Australian aborigines lived by – laws which offered much more humanity than those of modern Europe: 'Where there is punishment there is love. But the laws of a European are fearing. You are punished where there is no love' – were insistent on female submission.[1] 'Young girls who were causing trouble with their brazen behaviour were sometimes handed over to their husbands to quieten them down... Today young girls who are wild and offend are often given over in marriage.'[2]

For women, criminal behaviour has always been confused and conflated with their sexual behaviour, 'Next to murder', it seems, 'sexual waywardness was a woman's worst crime.'[3] Many old laws focussed on chastity and adultery, emphasising always, as in ancient Rome, that 'husbands were to rule their wives as necessary and inseparable possessions'.[4] In that other great bastion of early male culture – ancient Greece – 'respectable women', we are told, 'stayed indoors. In the law courts, a woman's having been seen at a banquet was frequently used to put her married status in doubt.'[5]

The much-vaunted courtly gentility of the Middle Ages did *not* extend to independent women. Independence was itself seen as a dire offence. 'A wife's lord in medieval Europe was her husband. If she killed him, this could be treason in English law and she could be burned like a traitor...he (also) had the moral and legal right to inflict corporal punishment on her: all law systems agreed on this.'[6] Onwards through the centuries, the law held on to one basic tenet: anything which threatened the security and sanctity of the family was to be severely punished. Adultery came to be known, quaintly, and moralistically, as 'criminal conversation', and in post-medieval times abortion and infanticide carried the death penalty throughout Europe.

Punishment for men and women was equal for equal crimes (although men certainly got away with adultery more often), with the one mitigating circumstance, where a woman might 'plead her belly': pregnancy.

The idea that women should be given softer treatment came only in the nineteenth century, mainly through the pioneering work of Elizabeth Fry, whose horror at conditions in Newgate Prison, England, led her to campaign for women to be housed in separate prisons from men, and to be offered rehabilitation (rather than pure punishment), such as gentlewomen's work: needlework, cooking, and domestic skills. Rehabilitation sounds humane. But its ramifications were far from that. Much agony has been caused since, by the well-intentioned social work of the likes of Elizabeth Fry. In theory, it means coaxing rather than coercion – based on an ill-advised and false conception that women must be protected from, rather than held responsible for, their criminal actions. In fact, society has translated that apparent concern for the 'softer sex' into doubly intransigent treatment. Nowhere was this more apparent than in America, the 'land of the free', which, in 1913, passed the Pennsylvania Muncy Act. An echo of nineteenth-century reform, the Muncy Act subscribed to the idea of feminine submission, and, in the belief that women were more receptive to rehabilitation than men, decided to leave women's sentences of indeterminate length – which often meant the *maximum* possible penalty – because women were seen to respond so well to institutional life! In 1908, Daisy Douglas and her lover, Richard Johnson, were arrested on robbery charges. Under the Muncy Act, Daisy was sentenced to twenty years – the upper limit for such a charge – while Richard, despite a far more serious record behind him, got away with a three- to ten-year stretch.

Such blatant injustice – later overruled by the Supreme Court – was carried on in different, equally insidious ways, through the twentieth century, up to the 1970s. Rehabilitation for criminal women was then replaced, in the psycho-pop world of the post-1960s social science boom, by the idea of therapy. This move had its roots in the much-vaunted criminological belief that women who commit crimes were doing so *against* their own sex, and therefore must be damaged goods, psychologically. A woman's appearance in court was

enough to warrant the idea of psychiatric reports on her mental state
and a strong emphasis on head treatment: psychotropic drugs and
counselling for mental illness. Holloway, Britain's largest women's
prison, was even redesigned in the 1970s, with the idea of therapy in
mind. As with so many brave new experiments in the wake of the
civil rights and radical movements of the last two decades, the money
ran out half way through. Holloway remains essentially unchanged in
its attitude towards criminal women – i.e. punitive – and even the
new buildings have never quite reached completion.

When I talked to women struggling nowadays with the definition
of 'criminal', and with the daily intrusion of cops, social workers and
courts in their disrupted lives, they stressed the *punitive* elements of the
legal world. It seems that we have gone back to very ancient
perceptions of women who break the law: that they are doubly as
culpable as men, and must be strenuously brought back in line. When
a woman stands in the dock, she is judged not just as an offender, but
as a sexual animal, a mother and a wife. When she goes on trial, it is
the idea of womanhood which goes on trial with her. As ex-prisoner
and campaigner Chris Tchaikovsky put it succinctly: 'I don't believe
these women are in prison for what they've done, but for rebelling
against their femininity.'

THE POLICE

The British police force have long operated according to a 'cult of
masculinity'. Their American counterparts do the same. It is a cult
championed in transatlantic television shows (see chapter 5) and
visible every day in city streets, as the panda cars zoom off, sirens
blazing, to catch some creature in the act, and to make themselves as
publicly visible as possible. Police attitudes to women are correspond-
ingly neanderthal. Forget the idea of female privilege – of handsome
beat boys protecting the flower of womanhood: the modern police

force can be fiercely misogynist, even towards its own kind. As Melissa Benn pointed out in an article for the Greater London Council's police-monitoring bulletin,[7] discrimination against women police officers starts with recruitment: there used to be an unofficial 10 per cent ceiling on female recruitment, and there are still very few women in the higher echelons of the CID (Criminal Investigation Department). In December 1983, WPC De Launay took the Metropolitan Police to court on charges of sex discrimination. She had been taken off duty in the traffic division because her senior officer feared that she and her male co-driver might be tempted to have an affair... The co-driver remained on duty. She won the case – after a brave struggle.

Another policewoman, who has now left the force, was sickened by the constant harassment by fellow officers. 'WPCs are called "plonks", good for nothing... Every time you come on the radio you're mimicked and insulted. I resented being called a "fucking cunt".' In such a climate as this, where women on the *right* side of the law are barraged with male abuse, it does not look good at all for those who step out of line, and are brought into custody.

Soft cop

Paternalism towards wayward women has always been used as a means of bringing them back into line. Often the intention behind such treatment is as stern as the upfront punishment of criminal men, but it is concealed in a surface fudge of kindly concern – so the malice is less easy to spot, the discrimination practically impossible to combat.

This kind of fatherly behaviour (one policeman told me that 'some officers' views are softened to females if they have a wife and daughter of their own') is doubly easy to inflict on young women – particularly those who are in trouble for the first time, and are probably frightened out of their wits by the uniformed impersonality of the police, and their bewildering routine.

Emma was barely in her twenties when she was taken in on suspicion of murdering her husband. She remembers kid glove treatment: 'There had been periods of questioning prior to my arrest, which weren't pressured, that I can remember. There weren't the sort of bully boy tactics you hear about. They more or less did the "We're-all-friends-of-yours-and-we're-just-trying-to-look-after-you" stuff. I was made to feel comfortable.'

Jenny also enjoyed rather gentlemanly behaviour from the police who came for her. Neither young nor impressionable, she believes the reason for their courtesy lay in her crime. She had been defrauding the post office in a sophisticated, long-term crime. Hers was a white collar offence – the traditional business crime – and as such a spurious respect was in order. 'It was very civilised. Mine was still the acceptable crime, you see. It was a crime that was very real to the people who controlled the court situation.' And when, after a year, the police had all the information they needed, they rang Jenny up, in a manner farcically close to an amicable business call: '"Well, we've got enough evidence. Could you find two people for bail, and would you mind coming to Bow Street?" They were *terribly* polite.'

Sarah experienced the same softly-softly approach. Middle-class, with an acceptably posh accent, her charge was involvement in an international conspiracy: top drawer material. So when the chief inspector arrived with his minions at 6.30am one day he was smooth and polite: '"I'm awfully sorry about this Sarah, but our friend C. has been up to a few naughty things. . ." I didn't feel under threat at all.'

This kind of treatment was far too good to last, and concealed a much more ruthless intention. As soon as Sarah was in the cell, everything changed. As so often happens to unwitting women (and men), she was bullied into signing away her innocence. 'Foolishly I allowed them to write down a statement – I did all the wrong things . . . Then when it comes out in court it's all slanted in a way that you hadn't meant at the time.' Meanwhile, the chief inspector continued to feign politeness: '"Sorry about this Sarah. You'd be surprised where our sympathies lie."' As the guilty verdict later confirmed – not with her!

As June also pointed out, polite behaviour from the police nearly always conceals an ulterior motive. 'They're nice to get information out of you – "Tell us about it and we'll be lenient" – and then they just hammer you.' And, as Marianne found, different sections of the police learn different tactics. 'There really are double standards. I mean the CID are a whole different ball game to the ordinary copper on the street. They can be very caring.' One even went to the trouble of making her tomato soup after a long stretch in custody – very different to the officer who went for her earlier in the day for being cheeky to a WPC. Marianne is under no illusions: careful treatment is as calculated as the less sophisticated bullying: 'The police now have learned to be much more manipulative and diplomatic in the ways that they talk to you – they've got to be much more careful.' This is because, as this book alone shows, the public eye is increasingly upon them, and popular opinion is ever more critical.

Hard cop

Hard cops do not mess around with niceties. Their treatment of suspect women is ruthless and frightening, and they will use any sexist prejudice or female 'weakness' in order to make their catch. Policewomen – themselves vunerable to male abuse – tend to be doubly punitive, as a defence mechanism. Says Mandy, 'The women are the worst. When I got done for shop lifting she came on like a Nazi in a concentration camp.' Mandy was stripped and then made to bend over. 'Did she think I'd got a pair of shoes up me crotch?'

The most obvious hold on women is the 'not bad but mad' conviction. Using the premise that all criminal women are psychiatric cases, the police often bring in mental health facilities as a means of enforced custody. Emma, who was at first treated so delicately, soon fell foul of her police father-surrogates. 'I had previously attempted to commit suicide, in the February. I poisoned my husband in the July. The following day, the police came to see me, and – I'm not claiming that any pressure from them caused this; I think it was simply the build-up of everything – I broke down quite badly by the end of the day. And they took me to a hospital. And from there I was taken to a mental hospital. Now I couldn't get out of that hospital. They wouldn't let me out.

'I've never been able to prove it, but I'm certain that that was the police. Because they didn't have any evidence to arrest me, they had arranged that I could not get out of this mental hospital, until they were satisfied, one way or the other.'

Did she make any attempt to leave? 'Yes, and they threatened me with a "section" (a legal means of having her admitted to hospital – a document signed by doctors and relatives, and invoked by the police or courts). I had supposedly gone voluntarily – in that a doctor from the hospital had said that I really needed this rest. It was only later that I realised it wasn't "a rest" – that there was something almost threateningly compulsory about this.'

The means she used to escape custody were desperate and drastic: 'What I did was fake an attempted suicide while I was there, and they took me to the Royal Infirmary in Newcastle. And while I was there they got a second opinion, which said that there was nothing wrong with me and that I could go. But I actually had to do that to get myself out of mental hospital.'

Annette had a similar experience when she was stopped by the police one night, distraught and dressed only in a nighty. She was in some mental distress, after losing a child and leaving her husband, who had been treating her very badly. Even though she was no longer living with him the police immediately informed him of her detention, and he had the power to have her forcibly committed to a private psychiatric hospital. She was there for six months, and was subjected to constant doses of largactil (a powerful tranquilliser) and damaging sessions of electro-convulsive therapy – a highly controversial treatment for mentally ill people. Those months are a blank space in her head, says Annette, but certainly taught her one thing: 'In this country there are still places where you can pay to have your relatives put away.'

Black women seem doubly at risk from the 'not bad but mad' tag. Under Section 136 of the British Mental Health Act, 1983, the police have a legal mandate to take a person from a public place to a 'place of safety' for up to 72 hours if s/he is perceived to be suffering from a mental disorder. At a Women and Policing Conference in London, October 1985, one of the papers explained that 'minority ethnic groups claim that the provision is used disproportionately against them. Do the police use Section 136 as a form of racial harassment? And are they mistaking culturally specific behaviour as signs of mental disorder?'

Drug addicts suffer similar discrimination, as Mary – a prostitute who uses her trade to support her habit – explained. 'I was always seen as disturbed and described as psychopathic and all that shit. One doctor said that whatever anyone did for me I kind of kicked them in the teeth. And I said, "Well, what's anyone ever done for me?"'

Coercion on grounds of mental health is often backed up by more obviously callous physical privations. Biological functions are an easy, inescapable target. So fastidious women are banged up in filthy cells. When Rebecca was locked in a shit-smeared cell she lost her temper for the first time: 'I said "You can't keep me in a fuckin' cell like this. You get me out." And they just slung a broom in.' Menstruating women are particularly humiliated. Rebecca: 'They make you feel bad. They love it if you've got a period – take the sanitary towel and rip it apart, because "something might be hidden inside".'

Drug addicts are particularly vulnerable, and in special physical danger – something police often use as means of extracting information, or simply as pre-trial punishment. When Marianne was on heroin, and was arrested, 'I didn't see a doctor and I was left for ages. And I was doing cold turkey really.' Anne, also a heroin addict, was treated badly from the moment of arrest: 'The police got there, got hold of me – now don't forget I hadn't had a hit, my arm was up like a balloon – they grabbed hold of me; they held me up the nick and threw me in a cell. They wouldn't give me a cigarette, nothing. They wouldn't give me sod all. I was shaking and everything. I said, "Look, I'm a junky" and they said "Just shut your mouth."'

Psychological tricks are often used to provoke an emotional response, and hopefully to incriminate the suspect. Emma, accused of murdering her husband, remembers a particularly unpleasant example. 'At one point I was given a book of photographs to identify. There were supposedly all round the house. In the middle, where I couldn't miss it, was one of my husband, taken in the mortuary.' She was never asked to identify this photo, and no reason was given for it being there. She can only conclude that it was there for one purpose alone: to shock a confession.

As with Rebecca, Jacki's memory of police holding cells is one of her most traumatic. 'I think it's the worst of the whole thing. It's like sensory deprivation.' All she could see was whitewash on the walls, one toilet, and one tiny window. 'It just drove me up the wall. I drove me mad.'

Her interrogation and police treatment was also intensely painfu Three officers confronted her: 'I was brought out after about an hou and a half to be interrogated. And this took about an hour. Then I wa put back in the cell and left there till that evening... When th ordinary cops came to feed me, they were just over the top. I thin they must have been instructed to treat me like that. They pushed th food across the floor. But I hadn't been misbehaving or screaming o anything. I'd just been sitting in this room.'

Jade had to use a cell opposite a disturbed woman every wee when she went to court, on remand – again a source of psychologica torment. 'All the time I was in this filthy horrible cell, she was in th opposite one going "Matron! Matron! Matron!" and she was goin "Give me one! Give me one! Give me one!" (a cigarette and a match) I later found out she was in for arson. They should have told me tha because if I'd had any matches, I might have given her one. In th police van she kept banging on all the windows to the people in th street. I kept my head down, I was so ashamed.'

Procedures of arrest are often manipulative or intimidating too When June was arrested, along with five men, they let her g initially. Because she was a junky she went straight for a fix, to calr herself down. They caught her again – this time in possession: doubl incriminated.

When women are arrested away from home it can make the mos legitimate of procedures possible sources of police harassment. June' solicitor and barrister were based in London, but she was on bail i Glasgow. 'One time I came down to see them I got done for breakin bail.' Mary, a prostitute, is permanently picked up in the street o soliciting charges – whether real or imagined. 'By law they'r supposed to see you approach three men,' she says, 'but they neve do.' This is a common occurrence for her: 'You're walking down th road, you could be soliciting but may not be. All they do is draw up i the car – "Right, in the back" – not "What are you doing? Where ar you going?" You know, there's no question. If you're there, you'r soliciting. So you get into the car, down the station, you're charged normally now they won't give bail for prostitution. Its very hard t get it, especially if you've got a lot of previous. They never ever give you a phone call.' (A detainee is supposed to be able to let someone know where she is.) 'They will call a doctor,' (she is an addict) 'but you've got to kick up a fuss. Then they usually take you to somewhere like Bow Street – what they call "holding cells" – for the night. They might give you cigarettes but they won't give you matches – and they won't give you a light. You're not allowed to smoke in the cells at all. A dirty mattress, dirty blanket. In the morning they come round to pick you up – take you to the cells under the court, where you have to sit for four hours in a freezing cold cell. Then you're just waiting, waiting, waiting to go into court.' Remember, she may just have stepped out of her front door to get a packet of cigarettes...

Not many people are aware of their legal rights, and women, picked up far less often for crime than men, are even less in the know. One crucial element in court evidence is the accused's statement. Although you do not have to sign anything, or speak one word, without first seeing your solicitor, many women *do* make highly incriminating statements, simply because they feel they must. The police play heavily on the vulnerability of ignorance.

Even June, who had been married to a criminal, and knew she could see a solicitor, 'because I was always doing it for him', was nonetheless hazy when it came to other rights, and ended up feeling 'I wasn't sure of anything.' Inevitably, 'I made a statement that was incriminating because I just didn't know that they (the police) were going to use it in that way.'

Jade was bullied into making a statement which also turned out to be highly incriminating: 'When my barrister looked through it, he was amazed, because they set up the questions very cleverly. The actual questions from the policewoman were very basic, and then he'd throw in questions – and you could tell which were his (the detective inspector). He was asking ones which would really incriminate you. They used a pronoun in a vague way. First of all they'd say "you", then "you" as a pair; then "they"; "him"; all different ones, so that quite a few of the same questions with different pronouns meant completely different things... Then they made me initial each comment and sign at the bottom of each page – and I couldn't read his writing. So I kept saying "What does this say?" and he said "Oh, just sign where I tell you." So stupidly I did. Easy life I suppose. It's amazing – people who haven't been in that situation can't understand. They say "Why did you say those things?" and I say "I haven't got a clue." I'd do anything just to get out.' The police officer in charge of Jade's case finally felt sorry for her naïveté, and rang a good solicitor saying, 'We've got a client who needs your assistance. She hasn't really got a clue what's going on.' By this time, however, the statement had been signed.

Rebecca was particularly scathing about the amount of invention on some police statements: 'Even the judge threw out the statements. She said it was impossible to have the amount of talking done in the time the police put down for interviews... When I saw him [the inspector] afterwards, I told him he should be a Hollywood script writer.'

The age-old discrimination of race and class is still used to the full by some police officers. As Marianne says, 'It depends on how you speak, how you're treated.' Seen by the police as a 'no hoper', as a young delinquent, Marianne – whose defiant lesbianism and tattooed arms turned them further against her – had some very rough treatment as an adolescent. She recognises the importance of class. 'When someone seems as if they're ... I won't say educated, but when they don't use jail-talk or are being militant – if you talk like you've got some savvy, and you're not gonna be pushed about, then it's a whole different ball game.' Anne saw through the class distinctions from the opposite side: 'Fortunately they're quite posh, my mum and dad, so they got a good lawyer in.' And she got off relatively lightly because of it.

Being black can weigh against you in legal practice. Olga Heaven, arrested in 1982 on a drugs charge, was sentenced to 3½ years, despite it being her first offence, and despite a good report from her probation officer. Other people were getting between six and 18 months for the same offence, but the judge told Olga 'I am going to make an example of you.' Why? could race have been a factor? It certainly was in the harassment of Mandy, a white woman living with a black man, who was told, 'You're just dirt anyway' because of her association with this 'spook', 'nigger'. When Agnes was arrested, her black girlfriend was hauled in too. 'They took her into the cells and gave her a bodysearch – because she's black; they didn't give *me* a bodysearch. And they really, really degraded her.'

At the 1985 Greater London Council conference on women and policing, Kim Black reported that 'Black women are frequently sexually abused by the police – and other people associated with the penal system'. No-one can forget the experience of Jackie Berkeley, who was raped in a police cell while two policewomen held her down. When Jackie made a formal complaint, she herself ended up on trial for 'wasting police time and tearing police shirts'.

Valerie Vaz, an Asian solicitor, commented: 'You never ever hear of cases of white women being virginity tested, which is why this struggle is something specific and peculiar only to black people... To think a government can produce legislation like that. To think it was a Labour government who produced the 1971 Immigration Act!' Part of this Act involves severe restrictions on entry from abroad, particularly for men, who are seen as a greater threat in the job market, but also for women. The virginity tests referred to here were introduced by immigration at Heathrow airport, and were used against Asian fiancées. According to official British thinking, no Asian woman had sex before marriage. So, if she wasn't a virgin, the logic went, she could not be a legitimate fiancée, and was not to be let in to the country. Heathrow officials regularly carried out vaginal examinations of Asian women to establish virginity – even though no physical test can prove this, and despite it being a gross act of sexual harassment and violation of personal privacy. The tests were stopped in 1979 when the *Guardian* blew the story and provoked a public outcry.

Finally, it is a matter of biology once again which offers the biggest pull for police over suspect women – this time in the form of children. Inevitably it is women who mostly care for kids, and since they are so dependent, the police have little difficulty forcing a capitulation by dragging offspring into the issue. A GLC bulletin, *Policing London*, stated in its November 1984 edition that, 'Women with children detained by the police are more likely to "give in" to the idea of a caution in order to get back to their homes, without being aware of the serious nature of a caution.' Women I spoke to confirmed this.

Says Mandy, 'They play on your emotions.' And Rebecca remembers being distraught when 'They came for me one night. I was on me own with the kids – my husband had gone out. And they just wanted to take me, with only a policewoman there for the kids...' Nor is the idea of court leniency towards mothers much in evidence, from what several women have told me. Mary: 'I remember one occasion when every single woman had children – was a single parent – and this magistrate was still sentencing them right, left and centre.'

The guilt which women always seem to feel towards their children is deeply enhanced by police comments and treatment. June's emotional response is one with which many criminalised women will identify: 'I feel so guilty – that they've still turned out so well after my fuck up; after all the damage I've done to them they still love me a lot... Even when I was a junky I told them every day, "Listen, I love you – I'm fuckin' up, but I love you." And they know that.'

Cartoon cop

Television has a lot to answer for. The modern vogue for over-dramatic cops and robbers series rubs off on the street – and the way some real police behave is better suited to the camera than to reality. Several women I interviewed had been arrested in true *Miami Vice* style.

Jade: 'They were following me in the car but I wasn't really aware of it. I took all the short-cut routes – they must have followed all the time. And just as I pulled up to some red traffic lights, this hand dived into the car, ripped out the car keys, and said "'Ere, we're from the drug squad, and we believe you've got drugs on you." Then he dragged me out of the car, put my hands on the boot, and then panicked because only one other police car had arrived... They were really nasty. They kept saying "Don't touch anything! Keep your hands in the air!" Then suddenly there were *masses* of cars. We caused a complete jam. It was really embarrassing. Everyone was staring... Finally they shoved me into the back of their car. The guy who was driving turned round and said "Better tell us now if you've swallowed anything, because someone died where you're sitting, last week." It was a guy who'd swallowed some drugs and they'd got really rough with him, so the bag burst.'

Less dramatic, but equally intimidating, was prostitute Mary's arrest for 'offending public decency': 'I was actually in a car with a guy and we were smoking a cigarette – I was doing business but we'd finished – just about to drive off when in comes the police van. He came up to the side of the car and said "Excuse me sir, would you mind opening your overcoat?" So the guy opened his overcoat and he was dressed, completely dressed... Finally we were in court, with a completely trumped up charge of offending public decency – because they saw nothing, nothing at all – I just couldn't believe how over the top they'd gone with their story. And when we got outside I said to the sergeant "You're just a fuckin' liar, you" and he said "Yeah, but you've got away with it plenty of times haven't you?": admitting that he'd lied.'

Prostitute Agnes, who worked from home, has had several consecutive run-ins with the police on various imaginary charges. Finally, as she was leaving the flat with a client one day – 'Just as I was turned the ignition on I was dragged out... "This is the police, Vice." I said "Shit, not you a-fuckin'-gain. What do you want this time?" He said "We're arresting you for a disorderly house." I said "Leave it out. What *is* a disorderly house?" And he said "What you've got 'ere, and this one you ain't gonna get out of." So I said "I wanna call my solicitor," and he says, "You ain't callin' no-one."'

Agnes was eventually convicted, but only after a courtroom drama in which her eminent barrister walked out of the case, insisting that the judge was biased against him, and against his client. This time, the cartoon cops had the last laugh.

Bitter isolation

Being arrested is not funny. It is a situation where a woman is subjected to intimidation, pressure, isolation and fear. Whatever she has done, whoever she is, when she is caught by the police and the courts, her humiliation is inevitable, the conditions she must endure, almost intolerable. When women talked to me about the loneliness and bewilderment they felt in police cells, and in the dock, that is when they touched on the very deepest emotions. Incarceration by the state is a terror we all feel. These women have faced its reality. That reality is pure pain.

Powerlessness is a familiar feeling for women. Nowhere do they face it more acutely than when in custody. Emma: 'I wouldn't say I was badly treated. There was even one policeman who, because I couldn't eat, specially made a bowl of soup for me. There *were* people who were being kind. But what was getting me was that the whole finger-printing thing wasn't being explained to me as it went along. I was just being taken to places and told "Sit there". I had no control over any of those things.' During the trial she was 'so far away that I wasn't actually feeling or thinking'. And the court structure did nothing to alleviate her dislocation. 'It's almost as if they deliberately design courts to make it difficult for you. I don't have a very loud voice – but even so, the jury are right down there; the person who's talking to you is over here; but the judge and the recorder are up there. Your instinct is to talk to the person who is talking to *you* – and so the judge kept asking me to repeat myself. This was starting to get to me – a sort of tennis ball effect all the time. It was almost as though everybody was pulling at you from every direction, but you knew the jury were right there in front of you, looking straight at you. Your confusion is trying to balance your head between all these people. It's *extremely* vulnerable, because you're up there on your own, and everybody in the room is looking at you. I found that I kept my hand up to my face' (a furtive-looking gesture, not designed to endear her to the jury) 'because I knew that my brain couldn't take in the whole body of the court.'

The dream-like quality of her trial has not become any more real with time and distance. 'My main feeling about it now is that it didn't happen to me. It is part of my history but I wasn't involved in it. It went on for four days and I really couldn't tell you anything that was said.'

Often women cover their confusion with a mask of hostility – again not a good approach for eliciting the jury's sympathy. Jade remembers: 'I never cried through any of this. I was very strong. It was as though it wasn't happening to me. I just accepted what was dealt out. You've got no control.' She became so bewildered in court – that 'I didn't know what the truth *was* any more. I felt as if it just wasn't happening to me.'

And when the verdict goes up – 'Guilty' – then the reality still seems oceans away. Agnes: 'I was just fuckin' numb. I couldn't believe it. And I thought to myself "What have I fuckin' done?"' Anne: 'I remember it, but it's like a dream to me now, a nightmare.'

Scathing comments from the police reinforce the attempts to undermine personal dignity and power. Adult women are treated like children. June remembers officers calling her a 'silly little girl – tut tut tut'. Emma can also recall being 'treated as a child. Though how much that's the fault of the police and how much it was because I was actually quite young, is hard to say. And it was a very traumatic experience, which tends to make you behave and feel quite childish.'

Many women are drugged to the hilt, which obviously magnifies the unreality of the situation and leaves them even less able to cope. Emma: 'They kept giving me tranquillisers when they thought I needed them. At that point I thought it was a kindness. But it meant I went through the whole trial skewed out of my brains, partly through the sheer trauma of it all, and partly through taking these things. I don't imagine if I'd had all my faculties about me that the result would have been any different, but I might have felt differently about it, might have felt I had more control over it, more say in it. But in fact I was so doped to the gills that I often wasn't answering, because half the time I didn't know what the question was.'

When I visited Barbara in prison, on remand, she told me she had drug doses three times a day. 'They won't tell me what I'm on', she explained, glassy-eyed, pasty and distant. Jacki was equally hazy about the medication she was given: 'The nurse in Holloway said on the first night, "You're down for this." "But I haven't seen anybody." "Well, you're down for it." So I drank it. I just didn't want to cause a fuss. I can see how people get marched to their deaths.' Unfortunately she responded badly to her mother's-little-helper: 'A lot of people like chloryl. It's like a double scotch. But for me everything *went*. I just buckled over. But it didn't stop me waking up fitfully at four in the morning thinking "AARGH! Where am I?"' As Emma said, 'The idea was, it would help you. It would stop you worrying. But all it did to was make me do it more slowly. It doesn't help you in any way to face up. All it does is distance you from the problem.'

One woman I spoke to, Karen, who has worked as a probation officer and a solicitor, is critical of the 'chemical straitjacket' used on women. *Anything* which blocks out subjective responses – and distances the accused from their own reality, precisely at a time when it is vital for them to be alert and in control – is disastrous. She says, 'It's really terrible that people are so reduced and humiliated by the court, to the point where they lose all sense of their own logic and well being.'

TRIAL AND ENDURANCE: THE COURTS

It is well-known that women in particular and small boys are liable to be untruthful and invent stories. (Judge Sutcliffe, Old Bailey Rape Trial, April 1976)

'No woman can be a criminal. To be a criminal one must be a man.'

'Now look here, what is this you are saying?'

'I am saying that you are criminals, all of you: the fathers, the uncles, the husbands, the pimps, *the lawyers*, the doctors, the journalists, and all men of all professions.'

They said, 'You are a dangerous woman.'

'I am speaking the truth. And truth *is* savage and dangerous.' (From *Woman At Point Zero*, Nawal El Saadawi, Zed Press, 1983)

Nawal El Saadawi is convinced of the innate corruption of male-dominated professions: professions which fundamentally seek to maintain the rule of men, and the subservience of women. Women working in the British legal system are no less severe in their criticism, and their political disapproval. Valerie Vaz, for example, an Asian solicitor, is under no illusions about her profession: 'I think justice in Britain at this time is an illusion, not a reality', she says – even though the basis of her training rests in the hallowed idea of objectivity and the correctness of law. But that same training drummed any idea of such legal purity out of her. She studied in the City of London – the world's legal mecca. 'That institution is male-dominated, male-orientated. It's very difficult to fit in if you're a woman. If you're a woman in the city, you're a secretary, not a solicitor. If they do accept you as a professional, you're seen as being there for a very short length of time and then leaving. They're prepared to use you – and admit that you're good – between the ages of 27 and 32. There's no prospect of partnership, no prospect of any kind of responsibility.

'When I was doing my articles, I was the only Asian woman there, and so I decided once I'd finished articles, that private practice wasn't the best place for me. I wasn't making an impact where it was really needed. And I wasn't interested in making money...' So she left to work for a London council.

Valerie is particularly appalled by the huge sums of money involved in administering 'justice'. Partners in firms of top solicitors can earn over £2,000 a week – more than the Prime Minister. Meanwhile working-class people don't stand a chance of affording to fight their case: 'The way things are going now – say on an immigration case – a lot of people can't afford to even speak to a solicitor.' She is sickened by the brazen injustice of this: 'The whole concept, when you're fighting for your rights, and fighting for your liberty, of having to worry about money, is ridiculous. It's *preventing* what the legal profession is supposed to be about.'

Within the court hierarchy itself, racial discrimination is apparent – and perpetuated by the public. Valerie: 'Often when I've been in the County Court, I've been mistaken for the court usher! People come up to me and say "Can you tell me when the next case is on?" It's always men who do that. White men.' The ranks are tightly controlled and closed to outsiders: 'Generally the law is very middle-class, and white-orientated. There's only one black high court judge. There's only one black woman registrar. There are lots of black people who are at the lower levels of the profession but almost none at the higher levels.'

Merle, a black barrister, witnesses corruption from the inside. 'By being part of the law', she says, 'you become above the law.' To many of her colleagues: 'You're either one of us, or, if you're not one of us, and you're in court, then you're a criminal.' Karen, a white solicitor, points out that from university training onwards, the law 'loses its whole humanity'. The prevailing attitude is that it's very important to keep the status quo and not question anything.'

The court's prejudice against women, black and white, starts early. Juvenile courts are much more likely to detain girls than boys for being in 'moral danger'. Delinquent girls are criticised for being 'unfeminine', as in a study from the 1950s by John Cowie, which talks of law-breaking adolescent girls as 'oversized, lumpish, uncouth and graceless'. Success is measured in insidious ways. Thus one tomboy adolescent passed through rehabilitation with flying colours, 'in record time, well-trained in domestic and social arts, to make a successful marriage'.[8] Rehabilitation, it seems, is about one thing only: being a traditional, passive female. The system, says researcher Maggie Casburn, is designed 'to protect girls from themselves. But it allows boys to be boys.'[9]

Girls, says Lesley Smith, suffer a double rejection when they are involved in crime: first because they violate legal norms and preconceptions; and second because 'in contrast to males whose delinquent behaviour is often seen as an extension of their role, these girls were seen to have offended *against* their own sex role.'[10]

This was certainly Marianne's experience. As an adolescent who was open about her lesbianism – and who also sported tattoos on her arm, which *no* self-respecting young woman would surely dare? – she encountered brutal censure from police in the north and south of England. Mary, too, experienced heavy punishment for her teenage absconding. She was eventually subjected to psychiatric treatment for her manifestly 'unfeminine' behaviour.

Writer Barbara Hudson maps out a frightening blueprint for court behaviour towards women – one which suggests powerful social control, far outside the rule of law itself. 'The very notion of "adolescence" and "phases" implies that current behaviour can be expected to be left behind as the phase ends and adolescence gives way to adulthood. That this is a realistic expectation is attested by a

dramatic fall-off in crimes committed by youths after the age of 17...
But femininity, after all, is something that girls are supposed to grow
into, not out of, so any signs of thwarted feminine development or
maladjustment to femininity will be treated very seriously indeed.
Intervention, both drastic and prompt, is thought necessary before
things get even worse... Women, for instance, are far more likely to
go to prison for a first offence than men are, and girls are far more
likely to be committed to residential care for a first offence than boys
are.'[11]

Later in life, the restrictions remain. The police are trained to see
single women as a deviation in themselves, as one article in a journal
aimed at the police reveals. Suspicious persons are to include:
'unescorted women or young girls in public places, particularly at
night in such places as cafés, bars, bus and train depots and street
corners.'

It is a popular theory that women are judged far more leniently
than their male counterparts. Certain members of the probation
services go along with that notion. Mr A., an ex senior probation
officer, certainly believes the leniency argument. 'My experience is
that courts are protective towards women and there is often a
genuine desire to help a woman defendant.' 'Help' often goes above
and beyond the call of duty, however, and some might call it
interfering. Mr A. again: 'I always felt that a woman officer could
bring an extra dimension in dealing with women offenders... matters
like child care, home-centred tasks; then use of makeup, choice and
style of dresses.' Would a man stand for explicit gender training like
this? He concedes 'that there is a logical reason for lighter sentences' –
their crimes are less serious, so the 'female sex appears in a much
more favourable light'.

It is certainly true that some courts are hoodwinked by their own
paternalist preconceptions, and some clever criminals do take
advantage of this.

Richard Ford, ex-warden of a bail hostel in London, does feel that
some women play on stereotypes to their own advantage. Amanda,
one of his clients, stabbed her boyfriend. While he was recovering in
hospital, she took up with someone else. Her probation officer
pleaded some mental disturbance, and she was let off, but Ford

maintains 'There's *nothing* wrong with Amanda.'

But as researcher Ann Smith points out, it is usually the case that 'Any special consideration given to a woman is given not because she is a woman, but because she is a mother, wife, or maintaining an elderly relative.' Not only the caring stereotypes are used for women, but also the ubiquitous sexual ones. Karen (solicitor) claims that 'There is complete sexual objectification of women in court – depending on how attractive they are.'

What happens, all too frequently, is not leniency, but a double punishment. Stepping out of feminine line is not appreciated in a society rigidly coded according to sex and gender. June was hopeful of an easy time in court, on drug offences. 'I was quite naïve. I thought I'd get away with it. I really did believe the whole thing about "You're a woman; you've got children", and a lot of the men who were charged out on bail had said that to me... And yet I actually ended up looking like this drug queen who had used men's heroin addiction to get them into dealing drugs from my house – which was total rubbish.

'When the judge was summing me up, I wondered who the hell he was speakin' about. It certainly was *not* me... They just made me out to be this monster drug person. And an unfit mother. I was feeling pretty guilty about that anyway, and they just hammered it into me: "How could you have done this to your children", etc.'

Mary is derisory of any attempts at soft treatment or rehabilitation. 'When I get nicked for prostitution, every time I've been in court I've said, "Look, it's because I use drugs", so they say, "Right – we'll send you to prison to help you get off these drugs." Huh! So you go to prison, they get you off the drugs, then you're let out the gate with £40... Nothing.'

Prostitutes are always vilified as 'common' – the lowest of the low. As Mary says, 'Being male, the magistrates always see you as bad – "wicked woman".' But it isn't just prostitutes who are portrayed as latter day Eves. Jenny, on trial for fraud, remembers, 'When the judge said that I'd wielded an "evil" influence over the whole courtroom – he hadn't said that to Michael, and I hadn't behaved any differently – it seemed totally removed from reality to me.' Her co-defendant, Michael was presented as the 'young company director', and the judge said 'He is obviously a Walter Mitty character who was carried away with the idea of owning all these businesses.' 'But *I* was the "evil influence".'

Other popular stereotypes are those of actress or liar or seductress (see chapter 5). Jacki had the misfortune of being an actress by profession. The prosecution had a field day. '"We see", he said, "that Miss Holborough spent 2½ years in *Crossroads* – pause, looks at jury – "Obviously a good performer!"' She remembers that 'my friends in the gallery heard one guy saying, "She's giving the best performance of her life."'

The special madness of UK immigration laws cannot in any way be said to favour women and men equally. A man settled in Britain may bring his wife in to join him. But a woman must be a British Citizen to bring in her husband, and that is a complicated and often costly procedure. This has led to grotesque trials, where women have been harassed, in order to prove that their marriage is one of convenience, just to avoid entry laws. The GLC *Women and Policing Bulletin*, July 1985, reports that 'immigration officers, working to the guidelines, have made enquiries about the couple's sex lives, read their letters, and said in at least one case that the letters were not affectionate enough for the marriage to be judged genuine!'

A report by Cambridge criminologists David Farrington and Allison Morris contests the idea that women are treated better in court than men. They found that divorced and separated women were actually handled more harshly than married women – and broken backgrounds were also frowned on. 'It could be', they say, 'that magistrates disapproved of these categories of women.'[12]

A Howard League Report on women in the penal system did not detect differential sentencing for men and woman, but found that 'women and girls who have engaged in what is described as "inappropriate sex role behaviour" receive particularly severe sentences'. Here again, medicine creeps in, on sentencing, as a means of control of women. Dr Bull, a former governor of Holloway, reported: 'We have a very large proportion of women remanded for medical reports, and a high proportion are negative, in the sense that there is no medical recommendation, and I think sometimes this is simply a device to put a woman in prison for three weeks, with the supposition that a medical report might do something, or perhaps just as punishment'.[13]

Commander Jenny Hilton of the Metropolitan Police Force admits that police and courts still operate on preconceptions, seeing females 'either as fallen women or angels'. As she says, 'either way you're dealing with stereotypes.'

Sometimes women *are* patronised in court – let off lightly because of the 'innate fragility' of their sex. Often they are not. Whichever way, women do not benefit from the prejudices of those who judge them. As Susan Edwards points out in *Women on Trial*: 'Women defendants find themselves, their families, life-styles and essentially their everyday conduct scrutinised, on trial, up for judgement, constantly surveyed by the various informal state mechanisms of welfare and the para-legal agencies. Scrutinisation and therefore control is more insidious, more complete, and more debilitating for the offender.'[14] In short, a woman is not allowed to get away with anything.

FINDING A WAY THROUGH

I no longer use my mind
Nor think of anything
For I am just a puppet
And my master pulls the strings.
There's one thing about it
I fear he doesn't know
Strings can be broken
And then he'll have to go.
(Young woman in youth custody, quoted by Gisela Konopka)[15]

When the long arm of the law reaches out for an individual, backed up by the full force of the state, there is little you can do to save your own sense of identity and autonomy. Women are particularly discouraged from defending themselves – their criminal act is already defiance enough. Solicitor Karen has found that in the courts 'women who assert themselves in any way are likely to be treated more harshly.'

However, some kind of psychological defence mechanism has to be used, because the choice in court, and then in prison, is starker than anywhere else in 'free' society: survive or go under. As long as justice is seen to be done, the legal institutions will not much care whether you come through or not. Ironically, it is usually by abandoning all vestiges of feminine 'vulnerability' that women in custody get by emotionally. June: 'I think in lots of ways with the police I did behave in a sort of hard manner – but I think that was purely fear; of not wanting to break down and grass anybody up.' Jade also remembers that 'I never cried through any of this.' Often a firm insistence on basic human rights does elicit a positive response. Unless you deliberately provoke the police – or they have a particular vendetta against you – then some sort of quiet compromise can usually be made. Thus, June 'refused to cold turkey. They got me a doctor and some valium and I just slept and slept and slept, and then they came and woke me up and said "Right, you can go now."'

Rebecca, a seasoned trouper in matters illegal, is also well-versed in the dos and don'ts of police procedure. Even when faced with a particularly stroppy officer and accused of the very serious crime of forging money, Rebecca did not give way. 'So he's sitting there with his Gucci shoes up on the table, flicking a bit of dust off his Italian trousers, saying to me "Well, that's it now. You're not getting bail, so from here you're going straight to Holloway." And I says to him, "Look I don't wanna talk to you – just take me back to the cell." A lot of people – women especially – don't know that they don't have to come out of that cell. They don't even have to say "hello" or "goodbye". They don't have to talk at all.'

Of all the women I talked to, Mary was the one most frequently harassed by the police and taken to court, because of working the streets as a prostitute. A fighter to the last, Mary always takes the opportunity given at court hearings to make a statement of her own. It is, she says, her one persistent protest against laws she finds unjust and unnecessary. Sometimes her protests even reach the public eye: 'There was a whole thing in the Gazette once, 'cos I wouldn't get out of the witness box. He was remanding me for a psychiatric report. I was saying "But you've got 20 years of psychiatric reports in front of you and nothin's changed. I'm still doin' it because I'm using drugs." He took no notice. The headline was "Prostitute says I need help not punishment".' But some magistrates do respond to the argument that arresting prostitutes is absurd: 'There used to be one at Marlborough Street who used to only fine you £5 – he just wasn't interested.'

Even the most inexperienced detainees learn the ropes very quickly. Jade, inside for the first time, on remand, remembers her initial reaction to Holloway: 'I put my head in my arms and I cried. Then I thought they might see me so I put on this really tough front.' She also learned to split matches to make them last longer – an essential skill inside prison – and also to unpick the staples on canteen bags (holdalls for belongings which you are allowed to take to court, but which, once opened, are not allowed back in prison with you). Jade was soon renowned for working the staples so that each bag looked untouched. Her skills were much in demand from the other women! Small tricks like this make for tolerable subversion of almost unbearable bureaucracy.

For some women, young and unsupported, a police cell is ironically, a far better prospect than a cold, friendless night. Marie, in trouble with the law since early adolescence, has a curious love-hate relationship with her captors. In earlier days, when she was practically destitute, she sometimes deliberately provoked arrest, just for the strange comfort of coming off the streets. As she says, 'I've done a lot of "criminal damage" just as a way of getting back inside because I've had nowhere to go.' She has spent much of her life inside, and says, startlingly, 'I didn't even want to come out of prison. I loved it there. The old hands would look after you, and teach you new tricks – really look after you.'

June was older than Maria when she ran into trouble, but was also quite confused and frightened with her life as a junky, and she reckons that 'in lots of ways it rescued me, being arrested'. Before it happened, 'It was like being in this hysterical laughter all the time – and in lots of ways I'm glad it happened 'cos it made me stop dead. It's rather an extreme way of doing things, and I'd rather not have done it that way, but too late, too late.'

There are organisations linked with the courts which do try to show women offenders a way through. One of these, in Britain, is the probation service, set up in 1907, to 'advise, assist and befriend'. These days it has an uneasy bridging function between sentencers and defendants, and reports made by probation officers can profoundly influence the outcome of a trial. If the relationship with a client is a good one, then it may continue long after the case is over, offering support – and a link back with the community – for those women who may be completely alienated by a stretch behind bars.

There are also hostels operating in Britain which offer temporary refuge for homeless women awaiting trial, or just out of prison. Richard Ford, ex-warden of a bail hostel in London, does not overestimate the effect of their work, since women on bail are in a kind of suspended animation, awaiting trial for their alleged offence, and thus not able to concentrate fully on creating a life and a future for themselves – 'We're an irritation between where they've been and where they're going' – but he is adamant that poor people should have a right to this kind of facility: 'You have the right to bail and the fact that you do not have a home or much money (two criteria used by courts to let you out on bail prior to your trial, rather than remanding you in custody) should not stop you getting that bail.'

Similar hostels and houses exist for women just out of prison. (They may well have lost their home base, if they had one, while serving this sentence, since landlords and local housing authorities are not very tolerant of tenants who are sent to prison.) Government and charity funded hostels alleviate the initial anxiety of 'where to go', and supply some security from which to start afresh. Janet Urry, a worker at one such house, describes its importance for people who stay there: 'For many of the women, a lot of their lives have been taken up in reactions to things, rather than thinking that they want to do things for *themselves*, and I think the function of this place is to give them the space to think about what *they* want to do. It's the first time they've not had pressures from other people, saying, "You have to do this, you have to do that", and reacting badly to all that. It's not always the case, but a lot of women here have had very bad backgrounds, and just haven't had the chances... It's about finding a better life, really.'

The problem, as always, is a lack of sufficient financial backing, to supply the facilities and personnel necessary to deal with the increasing numbers of women passing through the penal system. Bail hostels and the like are restricted in the kinds of residents they can handle, so offenders with more serious problems (like drug addicts, firesetters, or violent women) may not get a place. Even without these offenders, life in a hostel can be unpredictable and volatile, with women suddenly sharing responsibility not only for their own lives – possibly after years of a passive prison regime – but for the equally complex lives of other criminalised women. It is a great test of nerve and patience – for staff and residents alike. But as a way of disentangling difficulties over social security payments, homes and families, and offering non-judgemental support, these places are very valuable indeed.

There are also schemes – some state-run, some privately funded – which give practical advice on jobs to women coming through the legal system, and finding it hard to cope. Such back-up has previously been thin on the ground for women, who have constituted such an 'invisible' element in the world of crime. But work inspired by the women's movement throughout the 1970s has encouraged new awareness and, slowly, new facilities.

Apex Trust, a charitable organisation formed to help male offenders looking for work, has recently recognised the special problems which women suffer with employers – the fear of criminal women's innate instability, for example – and now has female ex-prisoners working with them, visitng prisons and also seeing clients outside. Similar facilities are offered by the Women Prisoners Resource Centre, set up in 1984 with a grant from the Greater London Council's Women's Committee, and managed by the Home Office-backed NACRO. The WPRC have contact with all eight penal establishments for women in Britain. They offer practical help on all basic 'survival' issues for women who have been sentenced.

But in recent years the most powerful voices raised in protest about the way women are treated in custody and in prison, and offering direct help to criminalised women, are those of ex-prisoners themselves. No-one can appreciate the agony and frustration of being a woman on the 'wrong side' of the law, unless she has been through it herself. In 1982 an ex-prisoner called Chris Tchaikovsky raised money from the Greater London Council and started a campaigning group called Women In Prison, which regularly visits women inside, and monitors conditions in all the women's prisons up and down Britain. WIP has a campaign manifesto, and regularly blitzes the press and the government with first-hand information about injustices inside prison, which would otherwise go unheard, unknown, unchallenged. It is an angry, effective pressure group, determined to bring about change, and determined not to let women inside remain invisible to the public eye. The Black Female Prisoners Scheme has now also emerged, to do the same, specifically for black women.

It is often maintained that committing crime can actually be an outlet for frustrated creativity. Jenny Hicks and Jacki Holborough have certainly proved this to be true in Britain, by setting up their own highly successful theatre group made up of women ex-prisoners. The Clean Break company has been touring the UK, Europe and America with sharply observed plays about women and crime since the mid 1970s. Through its workshops and performances, it has provided a creative 'clean break' for many women inside and outside prison. They also have links with CAST – Creative and Supportive Trust, set up by Lennie Spear in 1982 to give ex-prisoners training in textiles, silk screen, photography and pottery.

Glimpses of optimism like this are fantastically important for women who are used to the negative tones of police, judges, and prison officers. Probation officer, Jan, is adamant that although 'authority *is* monolithic and it *does* control your life – you *can* take some control for yourself'. Taking control is the philosophy she works from – imbuing her clients with some sense of their own worth. She despises the lethargy and passivity inbred by poverty, and by a technological culture which encourages less and less independence. 'Society', she says, 'engenders a feeling of helplessness in people.'

She has considerable success with the women she works with – due no doubt to her own determination not to give up on them. One woman, Rita, was a recidivist offender. She specialised in non-violent robberies. Throughout her probation she was difficult and demanding – asking for money, and, when refused, saying, 'Alright then, I'll go out and nick!' Then she insisted that her child be taken into care, 'or

I'll beat her up'. Jan recognised a spark of independence in Rita, however, and worked with her to bring it out. 'My relationship with Rita is significant,' she says. 'The energy was there and it was tapped.' Rita has now stopped offending, and has a healthy relationship with her child.

It's ironic, says Jan, that probation officers, and others who work in the same field, get assertiveness training as part of their job. But they don't need it – they are mostly middle-class, well-educated people. It's the clients who need it really, 'so I try to pass on some of that assertiveness to my clients'. Jan's article of faith – belief in people's own potential – is something more valuable to criminal women, and more likely to *de*-criminalise them, than any amount of punitive fines and sentences. If you really know and like yourself, the likelihood of casual offending becomes smaller and smaller, and the alternatives more promising, more creative. But it's hard, so very hard, in an increasingly depressed social climate, just to keep your head above water. And what must it feel like actually to be sentenced to prison – to be submerged into that whirlpool of broken hopes, slammed doors, and a trapped, fractured future?

CHAPTER 3

GOING DOWN: PRISON WALLS

If tears could build a stairway
and memories a lane
I'd climb the walls of Holloway
to be with you again.
(15-year-old girl waiting for transfer to Youth Custody Centre)

There can be no punishment more severe than the loss of one's freedom. (Jimmy Boyle)[1]

The thing about prison is that you are totally 'non'. You are nothing. You don't really exist other than as a body to be shifted from here to there. (Emma)

Prison is the other side of the adrenalin. (Mandy)

Imagine. Close your eyes and imagine. The smell of damp and urine. The feel of cold concrete under your feet and round your body. The confinement of one small cell. The hardness of one unsprung mattress. Food that may have been prepared by hostile male prisoners in another block, and comes to you foaming suspiciously, and tasting of sawdust. The constant glare of neon light. The ever-present echo of warders' keys, and heavy footsteps in the corridor. Total surveillance. Absolute isolation. The cries of women, mentally disturbed and physically sick. Dirty blankets. Cold nights. Unending days. This place has no escape – except in your dreams. Try very hard to imagine it – and then open your eyes to freedom.

That description is no exaggeration, and it is very close to home. You don't need to read *Gulag Archipelago* to hear stories of state cruelty and punishment – just talk to women who have been in British jails: Holloway, Durham H Wing, Styal, Cookham Wood ... Britain prides itself on being a civilised, liberal country (even though we imprison, for example, twice as many people as France, and four times as many as Portugal), but when it comes to women's prisons, it has a severely blotted copy book. Like America, with its female institutions, whose regime runs on so-called 'pastel fascism', Britain and Europe use prison to control, condition and condemn its inmates. Soviet writer Tatyana Mamanova says, 'It is well known that the conditions of any society are most clearly characterised by its prisons, barracks, and hospitals.'[2] There are differences between prisons round the world, but they all share one rationale – the punishment of people who misbehave: a grand sweeping-under-the-carpet of all irritants within the system. As far as the public is concerned, this technique is effective. Out of sight, out of mind. But the system's victims have a very different story to tell.

PURPOSE OF PRISON: THE SYSTEM AND THE STAFF

Institutions as they exist at the moment are a danger to the community. They simply harden attitudes and make prisoners more dependent by taking away all responsibility.
(Jimmy Boyle, *The Pain of Confinement*, Pan, 1985)

Before the nineteenth century there was practically no difference in the way society treated male and female prisoners. Sentences were the same, and prisons were mixed. Reformer John Howard was the first to create public disquiet about this in 1777, and his advocacy of single-sex institutions was furthered by Elizabeth Fry, a Victorian gentlewoman who was intent on making little ladies out of the inmates of Newgate gaol. The concern of these reformers was right in one respect; women *are* far less criminally minded than men – there are 1,500 female prisoners to 45,000 men in Britain; we boast just eleven female institutions to 123 male prisons – and women are generally inside for much less serious crimes than their male counterparts. The majority of British women prisoners are fine defaulters, or are inside for crimes against property, and drug-related offences. Violence against the person is not common. But in another respect, the do-gooders of the last century have handed down a dangerous and insidious legacy. In treating women as gentler, more vulnerable, biologically inferior, they paved the way for a confused and contradictory regime which on the one hand punishes women, and on the other hand patronises them, so that they leave under a double burden of helplessness and responsibility. As Pat Carlen showed, in her book about Scotland's women's prison, Cornton Vale, the inmates are treated like 'wee lasses'. One woman told her that 'Prison made us children again, and, when our term was ended, let us loose into an adult world.'³ Is this really the purpose of modern prison?

The daily round

The first taste of prison is usually confusing and alarming. Transferred from court room to prison in a police van, the new inmate first has to go through reception. Immediately she feels like an object, rather than an individual, and the various stages in the routine are rarely explained to a new arrival – making her feel vulnerable and exposed. Audrey Peckham, in her book, *A Woman In Custody* (Fontana, 1985) says, 'I remember odd fragments of my first experience of the reception procedure. Like being put into the tiny cubicle I later came to know as the "horse box" – for that is what it resembled, this tiny rectangular box measuring about two foot six by three foot with a piece of wood across one end to act as a seat.' After this, the prisoner is made to wash, her hair is inspected for lice, she is medically examined, and she must strip and twirl, to ensure there is nothing hidden on or in her body. (Stripsearches are repeated every time she enters or leaves prison. See chapter 6.) Her belongings are examined item by item, and the majority taken away for storage. Jade remembers in Holloway being allowed six pieces of makeup, six books and three sets of clothes; the rest was taken away. The new inmate may be put in a single cell, or with other women – depending on her offence, her health, and her behaviour.

There is a rigid daily regime inside British prison, for reasons of necessity – staff organisation, etc. – and of control. Things start up early in the morning, 8am or earlier, with slop-outs, washes, and the administering of medicine if necessary. Depending on how many staff are available, much of the day is spent locked up in the cells – sometimes 23 hours out of 24. Otherwise the day is taken up with cleaning cells, stairs and floors; exercising in the yard; working in education or sewing toys or mailbags for (tiny) wages. In the afternoon there is association between prisoners, the watching of television or the writing of letters. Lock-up in the cells for the night happens at around 8pm. The next day, it all starts again. Not exactly an invigorating, rehabilitative existence. But then there's always sleep...Except that the prerequisite for shut-eye of peace and quiet is never available inside prison. Individual rest is broken by all sorts of noises: night officers talking or patrolling outside; other inmates talking or crying in distress; the constant glare of institution lights. The daily routine is relentless – 24 hours a day.

The strict regime

It is hard to get an official statement from those in the prison service about *anything*, riddled as it is with a conspiracy of silence and secrecy, let alone to divine a coherent idea about the structure and purpose of the system. Governor of Holloway, Colin Allen, put a toe round the closed door at the beginning of 1986, when he held a public meeting in London about his prison. But all he could say in the way of penal philosophy was that, 'The job of a prison governor and prison staff is to *serve the courts.*' (And one prison officer backed this up when she answered a similar question about prisoners with: 'The judge says they've got to be there...') This essentially passive attitude is hardened by the very traditional and conservative attitudes of prison officers: the tangible human symbol of imprisonment. It is commonly felt that they – and not the governor – run Holloway, and most other penal institutions.

One reason for this grassroots dictatorship is the extreme pettiness of the prison regime, for *officers* as well as inmates. One prison officer told me disgustedly that, to the Home Office, their employer, 'You're just a number – like the women.' There are strict regulations about dress (caps to be worn at all times, and civilian jackets *not* to be brought into the prison) and habits (coffee to be drunk in one particular place only, and absolutely no deviations from the regulations).

Severity breeds severity: in prison it's an extreme case of divide and rule. One prison officer said dismissively of all prisoners, 'They're selfish. They're only out for themselves.' Another said, 'They're like children – they need strict discipline; to know what's right and wrong.' Holloway, she added, has one major fault: 'it's too soft'. But softness does not seem to be a word often used by those on the receiving end, and prison officers are seen as far more powerful than they themselves will admit. Ex-prisoner Chris Tchaikovsky: 'Unless prisons are open and accountable you can't do anything. You can insist on your statutory right to exercise or religion or whatever you like, but if the screws don't want to let you do these things, you don't do them.'

So the charade goes on: rigid uniforms – as one prisoner put it, 'Symbols of the fact that they are not like you' – big bunches of keys, and an insistence that they be called 'Miss'. 'How they see themselves', says Emma, 'is not the reality... They don't want to see the reality... because if they did, the whole thing would crumble.'

Rather, the ugly nightmare that Emma went through for six years, wearing blue knee-length regulation knickers, years old, and yellowing with age, which it took a male governor to banish, despite constant reports of thrush among the women. 'There's something', says Emma, 'that says "I'm not you" – even down to the knickers. It makes them feel better. It bolsters their ego.' Similar restrictions are placed on literature. Any 'subversive' books are banned, leaving, as Barbara says, the Barbara Cartland variety – 'virgins in white dresses'. Visitors are messed about too. On the numerous visits I made to Holloway, I was faced each time by a different rule about prisoners' gifts: screw tops or no screw tops on bottles, that was the question. And it depended on the officer in charge as to what was allowed in and what refused.

Not all prison officers are rigid figures of authority, walking around 'like John Wayne', as Jacki quaintly described one notorious character – and the prisoners themselves do see a need for them to be around. June: 'OK, there's nothing wrong with the job itself. I believe it has to be done. But it's how you do it. You can personalise it a bit. There are officers who do care about you that little bit more; who know the regulars who come in and out; who'll come and talk to you at your hatch when you're feeling down n'all; put your arm around you. And there are the others who won't.'

The spark of humanity between prisoner and warder is rare; when it happens, the moment is sweet. June again: 'There was a security officer who everybody disliked. Now they thought I had such cheek, because I applied for the gardens (a plum job). And I got it. And she came up to me and said, "Now don't let me down – I've taken this on my back, so don't let me down." And I liked that woman from that day – that she was prepared to take that risk. Yet she was never a friendly woman. She was always the first one to punish you if you messed around. Didn't smile much – but once she did that for me, there was this little twinkle in her eye. And I thought, "Yeh," you know? "You're alright."' It is a terrible thing – women locking up other women, setting themselves apart, and brandishing the rod of brutality and superiority. And yet, as June says, 'I think it should be a caring job. A lot of the women in there need to be cared about – that's why they're in there.' All too often the *lack* of care is almost arrogant. June: 'They're too ready to hear bad things... Often they're right. They'll say, "Oh, she'll be back," and I think that's wrong. Even if they *are* goin' to come back, don't say that – don't reinforce it. Jus' hope that they won't.'

Even so, many officers refuse to see their own collusion with the system. Says Emma, 'All the time there is this dichotomy between reality and their image of themselves. They see themselves as kind and caring and supportive, and "We're only here for your good, dear" – as they slap you in a padded cell and lock the door on you for a week; as they lock you in ten minutes early because they want a coffee break; as they lock you up for a whole day, because they really can't be bothered letting you out...'

Because of the loneliness of the average prison regime, prisoners are thrown back on each other for support. Sometimes this support is emotional – that of a close friend – and sometimes it is physical too. Lesbianism is common in prison, and apart from being a legitimate sexual choice, acts as a tender and logical way of combating the bitterness of personal isolation. Prison authorities feel threatened by such demonstrations of closeness. Wherever possible, they break them up. In Britain there is even something called the Lesbian Activity Rule, where, as Lynn Barlow explains, 'You are not allowed to sit on the same chair, bed, etc., alongside another woman.' Once, when playing cards with a friend on her bunk, she was reported under this ruling. Inevitably women are scared of forming friendships under these circumstances. They remain lonely, isolated, punished.

Pastoral care: making a proper woman of her

> Some day the thing I have dreamed must come true. Prisons will be transformed, changed from a prison to a home. (Madeleine Doty, Prison Reformer, turn of the century)

The legacy of Elizabeth Fry is everywhere apparent in prison. Despite the obvious inhumanity of cells and locks, barred windows and metal bunks, penal establishments take great care to remind women constantly of the compulsion and need for 'femininity'. If society itself is backward in its attitudes to sex and gender, then prison, that stinking carbuncle on the social backside, is even further behind. Pat Carlen believes that the reason for most women being inside in the first place is all bound up with being female – and sinning against it: 'For the majority of these imprisoned women have not merely broken the law. As women, mothers and wives, they have also, somehow, stepped out of place.' The Scottish sheriffs, she says, concentrate on women defendants' success or failure as mothers – and punish accordingly. What hypocrisy, she feels, in a regime which breaks up homes, and then concentrates on inculcating domestic values! This feminisation of prison is blatant and ridiculous. The main block of Scotland's Cornton Vale is called 'Papa'; wings of British prisons are called 'houses'; association areas are 'sitting rooms'; the main syllabus emphasises home economics and child care. All this, while many women are in enforced separation from their children and families.

Audrey Peckham, in her book about remand in Pucklechurch, recalls the infantilisation which went along with this notion of femininity. On Sundays they would all gather for religious service – and the music was children's hymns and tunes: 'I recognized this as an attempt to recreate the atmosphere of Sunday school, or perhaps infant school, when things were safe, before they had become disillusioned and their lives had begun to go so terribly wrong.'[4]

This is an interesting comment because it describes a dual process: women craving safety (and thereby abdicating power) and the prison regime fostering that process. Surely the system's aim should be to build prisoners up to face things outside *better* than they did before, not worse?

Sometimes the pastoral care image becomes a parody of itself. Emma remembers one governor's keenness to build up the 'community spirit', which in this case meant a fake ornamental pond and an invitation to the Salvation Army Band, which came in to play to the assembled, faintly incredulous inmates. All in all, says, Emma, 'prison staff have very traditional perceptions of women and a woman's role. And if you don't fit that role, you set up an antagonism that permeates through.'

Race and class are issues of contention in the same way. If the regime is reactionary about women, then it is doubly negative about women who are black and working-class. One black woman who was in custody for two and a half years reckons that 'there is a lot of racism from prison officers, teachers, the lot, but mainly from the prison officers. The attitude has come down from the Home Office... They try and keep black women prisoners separate, whether a black girl is conscious of her colour or not. They'll put one black girl among 30 white girls. It's common practice in Holloway...About two thirds of the black women prisoners are drugged. In prison there's a system, and if you don't play it they beat you up and attack you, and if you're black you get more pressure, because you are not only fighting for your prisoner's rights, you're fighting for your black rights.' June, whose skin is relatively pale, escaped the sharp end of this treatment. 'I wasn't *that* black so I wasn't that much of a threat. White enough to be acceptable. Straight hair. I think if I'd had "negro" hair I'd have been put somewhere else, categorised in some other way.'

The resentment *she* caused was not through colour but intellect. It seems the prison can cope with inarticulacy – the working-class woman in her place; but when that woman learns to speak up, she causes consternation. Up in Scotland, Emma found that too when she embarked on extended study, and June remembers: 'A lot of officers resented someone like me getting the chance to get an Open University course. I was very articulate and some of them (the officers) were so dumb. I used to tear them to pieces and they'd just stand there. I used to get my kicks that way.'

The only way the prison system can cope – as it is, after all, primarily about *containment* – is by putting all women into neat little boxes, painted pink, and leaving them there. Marilyn Haft: 'The women are treated like children, and even elderly prisoners are referred to as "girls". The psychological oppression has worked to such an extent that few women in prison have the sense of political consciousness possessed by many of their male counterparts, nor do they have confidence in their ability to help themselves legally or socially. Their ghastly self-image is consciously reinforced by the condescending boarding school atmosphere.'[5]

Punishment: beating the rebel out of her

> You who sit out there, what the fuck do you know? How can I expect you to understand what it means to be in the control of people who look on me as an animal? (Jimmy Boyle)

Very few independent bodies can find anything useful about the prison system as it stands. The Howard League, a British penal reform trust, goes so far as to say that 'There is too much about it which is neither just nor right: there is even more that is absurd.'[6] The plight of women in prison is even more absurd. Many of them are locked up on derisory charges, which sometimes come to public attention – like the young woman banged up in Holloway in 1986 for stealing a bottle of milk! – but all too often remain hidden, pitiful statistics. When the Howard League did a study on women in prison, they reported that 'Governors, prison officers, probation officers, educationalists and ex-offenders all agreed that very many of the women in prison ought not to be there.' Women have less money than men – and are less able to pay their fines; they are often put inside on first and small offences – often for offending the judge's notions of appropriate female behaviour. In short, their crimes are minor. To put them inside, even on a charade of 'pastoral care', is insulting. But what is worse is when that surface paternalism breaks down. Underneath, the reality is cruel.

In obedience to a system bent on punishment, prison officers are capable of inhumane and degrading treatment of their charges, and, as Emma says, 'the sad thing about this is, it's women doing it to other women.' A Home Office report by NACRO published in January 1986 showed that 'women prisoners are punished for disciplinary offences twice as often as men'. In 1984 there were 3.3 offences recorded per head of the female prison population, to 1.6 for the men. It is well known that women react more fiercely to confinement than men. Often they have more to lose – children and families – but they are also reported as having more *character* – as one probation officer put it, 'the men are more like sheep'. Certainly, any rebellion they do make is quickly and firmly quashed.

The most popular method is drugging – the 'liquid cosh'. There is an alarming disparity between the treatment of men and women, as the 1982 drug dosage rates for Britain reveal. I looked at statistics for two London prisons, one male, one female. For psychotropic (mind-altering) drugs Holloway – with a population of 350 women – records 212 doses per woman per year. Pentonville – with 960 inmates, over three times as many as Holloway – records just 25 doses per man per year. The same gap appears for hypnotic drugs – Holloway 62; Pentonville 2. Total dosages come to 365 per head for Holloway, and just over 50 per head for Pentonville.[7] No wonder most of the women I visited looked so glassy-eyed. As Colin Allen, Holloway's governor, pointed out, women *outside* prison are also far more susceptible than men to being prescribed tranquillisers and other controlling drugs. So what prison does is highlight and magnify the artificial means society uses, to literally keep its women quiet. And as a psychologist who had worked in Holloway told me, the staff are certainly drug-happy: 'They tend to try people on one thing and if that doesn't work, they try something else.' Jenny Hicks remarks drily: 'One woman went in for importing cannabis. She came out addicted to largactil.'

Sometimes the cosh is not liquid. Although one prison officer I talked to was adamant and genuine in her insistence that they do *not* hit prisoners, women's own stories are different and startling. This excerpt from Andrea Freud Loewenstein's prison novel *This Place* gives the flavour of several real-life stories I've heard. Telecea, a black inmate, has been causing trouble. Candy, the narrator here, sees just what will happen next. 'Moody would round up three or four more men screws, and they they'd bunch up and come charging in like it was some big badass riot. . . When they saw it was just Telecea they'd be all let down and take off her clothes and beat her up good, since they wasn't allowed to kill nobody here. . . They was like sharks that loved the taste of blood and would hurt a wounded person more. . .'

Anne's memories of prison violence are hardly less disturbing: 'I've seen them cart this skinny bird off, and if she don't shut up by the time they've got her to the cell, they strap her up and give her a couple of boots, but always where you can't see it. . . And then say it happened in the struggle. And you can hear them saying "You dirty whore, you little shit" and all this.'

But the cruelty is rarely so blatant. Subtler methods of control are used, designed to exasperate the prisoner into some kind of reaction – a reaction which brings further punishment. Emma remembers the months of anguish she went through in quest of parole: 'Prisons aren't above that you know. They do set up situations to test how you can cope with them.' These can be major – or extremely petty, as Mandy found out when officers deliberately withheld a birthday card for her, sent by her husband. A small incident like that was enough to send her berserk with frustration – and get her put on report.

The systems of remand and parole are examples of extreme bureaucracy, often used to exacerbate mental tensions in prisoners. Women on remand are untried, and unconvicted, yet they are locked up like other prisoners, and indeed often suffer worse privations, due to lack of staff and overcrowding. In Britain there are far too many women on remand, given the eventual conviction rate. In 1983, out of 3,292 women on remand *less than one third* were given a custodial sentence. Loss of liberty like this cannot be made good.

Parole is equally agonising. This is the means by which prisoners gain remission of sentence, by application to the appropriate board, and on proof of 'good behaviour'. Says Emma, 'Parole is used as a control method. It's used quite openly and it's used very subtly.' She waited three years and eight months for her parole to come through, and 15 months for the initial response to her application: 'Your only goal, your only reason for living is to get out of there – and to keep you waiting for 15 months... Anyway, when they *did* say to me "Oh yes, you can go", it was for two and a half years time. To my mind that's nothing short of mental cruelty.'

Medicine: a fatal neglect

No-one would deny that medical care in prisons is woefully lacking. Colin Allen, Holloway governor, admits that 'You might well say that there is insuffient medical support.' One major obstacle to improvement, certainly in Britain, is that the system is *not* run by the National Health Service, but by an autonomous body, the Prison

Medical Service, which is answerable only to the Home Office, and is, of course, top secret. The lack of sufficiently trained staff means that women are often at the mercy of prison officers, who use lay knowledge to assess often highly complex situations.

At one point during her sentence Emma was on the point of cracking up. Her weight plummeted to five and a half stone. But the warning signs went unacknowledged. 'The problem is that the officers are not qualified. They don't know. They can't identify when you've gone too far. And the psychiatrist only comes once a week. If you crack up on a Monday, you just get put in a padded cell till he appears on Friday. If they are making a misjudgement they can't know till he comes in on Friday. You could be dead by then. You could have mutilated yourself.'

Not only do staff lack the expertise to cope with prisoners' medical and psychological problems, they sometimes leave other inmates to face the inevitable outbursts of pain and crisis. Jenny knew someone in Styal who was left alone with a disturbed woman on her wing: 'Then you're forced to cope not only with your own prison sentence but to cope with someone cutting up. She had to sit for hours with someone who was bleeding. The screws knew she was bleeding and decided to leave her there for three hours – but this other woman had to cope with her.'

The psychiatric wing in Holloway, C1, receives continual bad publicity because of inadequate nursing of its women, women who should be in hospital, not prison, and who show their distress regularly by headbanging, and severe self-mutilation. C1 is known ominously, as the 'Muppet Wing'.

Even straightforward medical problems are ignored and exacerbated. A woman visited by campaigning group Women in Prison had been complaining of bad teeth for months. She was left for so long that eventually all her teeth had to be removed: an operation vastly more expensive and painful than simple, humane prevention. Jacki Holborough is derisory about doctors' treatments when they *do* arrive. In a play about Durham H Wing, she writes, 'The doctor thinks that a handful of multi-vitamins will cure our third world diseases.' Simple measures – like proper food, and human sympathy – would alleviate so much of the anguish for women inside. Too often, neither is forthcoming. Mary remembers a woman of her wing crying out in the night. She had just been forced to give up her child for fostering, and suffered recurrent nightmares. In her abject distress she was told repeatedly by staff to 'shut your mouth'.

Sooner or later this kind of human neglect will have fatal results. Deaths in prisons are a highly emotive subject. There has been much publicity over male fatalities but not so much over female tragedies. Women in Prison keep a dossier on women who have died over the last few years. They have all gone under in distressing circumstances, and it's hard not to feel that many of these instances could have been avoided.

In 1980 Julie Potter, aged 21, with an IQ of only 69, said that she wanted to die, and would set herself alight. She was transferred to a segregation unit, where matches were forbidden – and rightly so. But the very next day she was returned to the main body of the prison. Here she was left alone – *with* matches. Soon screams were heard. It took eight minutes to open her cell door. Too late. She burned to death.

Marie Zsigmond hanged herself in her Durham cell on her fortieth birthday, in despair over the killing of her son. She had repeatedly requested psychiatric help, which was refused.

In 1983, Joyce Marsh, an epileptic, was found face down on her bed in Styal prison one morning. No-one had noticed the danger during the night – and the night duty officer 'is not allowed to unlock cell doors on her own'. Checks were made through the windows – but was this adequate?

Sarah Hewer died in Pucklechurch Remand Centre in January 1985 after being refused access to a doctor by the prison nurse, and after ringing her emergency bell all night long. She had been left for ten hours, struggling for breath, and was being dosed with antibiotics possibly harmful to her condition. Sarah was 21, and had been remanded in custody for stealing goods worth 66 pence.

These are just a few victims of the system. Whether they deserved to lose their liberty or not, they certainly did not deserve to die.

EFFECT OF PRISON: DESTRUCTION OF THE INNER SELF, AND THE SILENT SCREAM

Chaos, anger, pain

Speak not so loudly
For I am in pain
Your voice's sharpened edges
Are cutting my brain.
(Larry Winters, quoted by Jimmy Boyle in *The Pain of Confinement*)

I know not whether laws be right,
Or whether laws be wrong,
All that we know who lie in gaol
Is that the wall is strong;
And that each day is like a year,
A year whose days are long.

The vilest deeds like poison weeds
Bloom well in prison air
It is only what is good in man
That wastes and withers there.
Pale Anguish keeps the heavy gate
And the warder is Despair.
                    (Oscar Wilde, 'The Ballad of Reading Gaol')

Whatever the purported intentions of prison, the effect on its victims is always one of pure anguish. Jenny remembers her entry into confinement: 'The first few days were the most dreadful – the reception process; those horseboxes; women in all different states of trauma, shock, drug/alcohol withdrawal and just plain illness – having been in police stations for days without being able to bath or wash; getting in the bath with a few inches of water and an officer standing there; not knowing what's what; not knowing when they're gonna come for you... It's a confused chaos, humiliating and degrading at the same time.'

The worst thing of all about going to prison, besides the squalor, is the sudden, brutal loss of freedom: the most basic and essential human right. Jacki, a non-violent offender, was sent to Durham H wing, a high security jail: 'I'd been free just a few days earlier – walking around and going into shops, and suddenly I was in this place where there were three sets of bars at the windows, cameras, and floodlights and spotlights and barbed wire. I just laughed and said "Who do they think I am?"'

The absolute cut-off from society is particularly hard on foreign women, who may not even share a common language with their captors, heightening their fear and isolation. Immigration cases are the most vulnerable, as Pauline Wilson explained at the Black Female Prisoners Conference, London 1985: 'Women who end up in prison are invariably trying to eke out a better lifestyle and living, both for themselves and their children, therefore the issue of immigration on charges of smuggling poses added problems for us. A number of sisters who are detained entering the country from third world countries would have left their children there and might not have made concrete arrangements about their care. Therefore it is understandable that it is more stressful for them to be in prison, on top of being thousands of miles away from family and friends.'

Once again, children add a sharp edge to the confusion of prison. It is the most bitter feeling of separation; one eloquently described by many of the women I spoke to. June summed up the intensity of loss for all of them: 'That was the worst thing that I ever felt in prison – being taken away from my children. I wish they'd chopped me arm off, or chopped a leg off, or taken one of me kidneys out – anything rather than that. That was the most painful thing – my womb used to actually ache. I'd sob and hold my belly. The pain – physical and emotional – of just not having them with me.'

Violence done against you breeds violence within you. Many ex-prisoners – women and men – talk of the training ground for aggression which prison has become. It is a survival mechanism. It is a final, desperate strategy for self-respect. Jenny hit out at a woman for the first time in her life when she was inside. Luckily she was enough in control to stop the punch and analyse the feeling. Many other women are not so fortunate. In Jacki Holborough's play about

Durham jail, *Decade*, the main character hisses ironically, 'I've got more hatred now than when I first arrived', and Mary is aware that 'It's taught me to hate so much that it's frightening. It's tried to destroy every bit of humanity I used to feel. It's left me feeling empty – too frightened to feel anything for anyone. As a close friend said of her experience, and it's exactly how I feel myself: we don't know how we feel, whether we want to cry or laugh – its just emptiness for us.' Rage, rage, rage. June's mask of survival was set before she'd even arrived in Holloway. 'By this time I got there and sat down, I was like a hardened criminal... Aggression has a lot to do with it. My kind of aggression was very quiet and silent. I'd talk a lot but you could feel a rage all the time, I'd make sure of that. And there *was* rage, and anger there, that could, at any time, spill over onto somebody else.'

There is, in women's prisons, as Audrey Peckham remembers, 'a barely suppressed violence in the air', 'a serious temptation... to hit someone very hard indeed'. Sometimes the tension is so great that the ultimate violence takes place – self-mutilation. Taught to hate themselves sooner than anyone else, women find it easy to turn inwards and strike at their own souls. The stories they tell of these moments are harrowing, humiliating – an indictment of us all, for letting it happen. This letter was smuggled out to Women in Prison. 'You made me really embarrassed by telling me to pull up my sleeve to show you the cuts I'd done. I hate looking at them and I feel ashamed for doing it now. But at the time it's the only way to let out the way I feel. I just slash them without thinking. I don't feel the pain at the time. It's later when I can't stand it. The cuts start to swell after a while, so by the time the doctor gets here they're really sore and tender. They don't use an anaesthetic so it's agony. The last time I had them stitched I went all dizzy. My ears were burning and I couldn't see. I felt terrible. I know it's stupid to do it in the first place, but I'd rather leave it open than get stitched and go through that pain all over again.'

Creating a zombie

> As I crossed the inner courtyards I could glimpse the faces of the
> women, lurking behind the iron bars like animals, their white or
> brown fingers twisted around the black metal. (Nawal El Saadawi,
> *Woman at Point Zero*, Zed, 1983)

Prison's unique form of reductionism does much to pull humanity
down to its lowest level. The image of women peering like animals
through steel bars is haunting and appropriate. Contrary to what the
law and order brigade would have us believe, prison rarely
encourages moral muscle, but instead compresses intelligence into a
downward spiral. It encourages the creation of animal-like, dumb-
witted automatons. Says Emma, 'The idea is to have a whole squad of
little non-people – almost like zombies. That's how they would
actually like you to feel.'

Ex-prisoner Jimmy Boyle describes this feeling of total, blind
impotence as 'the silent scream' – a flash of inner terror which hits
you when the full impact of incarceration finally sinks in. Jane
remembers a similar sensation: 'Yesterday I was walking up the stairs
to my landing and suddenly I had a terrible desire to scream. I
thought, I must stop now and scream – let it all come out. But then, as
I shook on the verge of action, I thought, what will happen to me if I
do let go? Of course I shall be dragged away.' Her scream stayed
silent, the terror locked inside.

Part of the stupefying effect of prison is the self-acknowledged
need to hold onto your feelings, for fear of further punishment. Says
Emma, 'You spend a great many of your years controlling your
behaviour rigidly.' This dual restriction cuts you off from the real
world, and, as Jenny says, is 'an alienating, isolating experience'. But
you are forced to go along with the alienation, or go under. Mandy:
'You have to cut off from the outside and concentrate on being
inside.' She set her mind on two years of this – like a permanent shot
of novocaine – and until her release, simply *endured*.

Whatever pressure there is to let go of these pent-up feelings, is not
used in a therapeutic way, but as a further means of control. Prison
officers are encouraged to elicit confidences from inmates – secrets

which are all too often turned against them. Emma, a long-term prisoner in Scotland, considered this subtle coercion a particular strain. '*Every* conversation was monitored. Staff hid in corners to listen to you. I mean I've caught them at it – lurking at the bottom of the stairs listening to what was going on. I actually walked out of the sitting room one day to find a screw tiptoeing round the corner – her ear up against the wall. They also have an intercom system (for contacting them in the night). It's got an on-off button, but it doesn't work. You're ON all the time. They won't tell you that – we discovered it from a member of staff who disapproved of it.'

The combination of surveillance and isolation is sometimes alleviated by friends, but this interaction is often strictly controlled. Mandy was in Styal prison and remembers bitterly, 'If you make a friend they take them away from you.' So what is left? Numbness. Mental paralysis. Jade: 'For the first few weeks I didn't really think I was there. I just lay on the bed and didn't sleep at all. I just stared at the ceiling – and kept ... aring this awful wailing from the psychiatric wing nearby.'

The high technological equipment of modern prisons makes the whole experience even more removed from human life, as Jane remembers vividly. 'When they first brought me in, through the many sets of electronic doors from the outside world, I just had to stand and gape. The narrow wing seemed to go up and up, four landings in fact, and not a soul to be seen – just a strange hollow silence. And there was this glare, like something somewhere in space. Yes, that's it, I thought I was on a spaceship. It took a while to adjust. The glare was produced by the most clinically clean and shining surface I'd ever seen, lit by rows of bright fluorescent lights.' The unnaturalness of the surrounding divorces you from any sense of yourself as a free individual. As the Judith Ward character says in the play *Decade*: 'I live here in this artificial light. This is where I'm always going to live.'

As the weeks go by in this giant goldfish bowl, a prisoner's grip on reality becomes feebler and feebler. Emma: 'If you're in there for six months you can say, "Oh bugger it, I can stand this," and you can make your little adaptations. But if you're in there for a long, long time, those adaptations go a lot deeper and become permanent. *You actually see prison as reality, and life outside as the dream.* So all your social skills, all your mechanisms, are geared towards prison. And of course when you come out, they're not valid any more.'

The menial daily round of prison unhinges any independent streak in long-termers. Social reformer of the early 1900s, Mrs Cecil Chesterton, describes the process as one of insidious mesmerism: 'She is, as it were, hypnotised by an unending submission and has lost even the desire to break her bonds.' The prisoner becomes used to cleaning floors over and over, till they shine with an unearthly gleam. She performs the most boring, mindless tasks in endless repetition. She is trained for nothing but submission.

Black prisoners are often pushed to the bottom of the ladder. As one woman remarked, 'The authorities say they offer us a chance to develop a career, so that we can become "dutiful citizens of society", but we are not allowed to use the facilities to their full potential; all we do is make doctors' gowns and do menial jobs, or we are banged up in our cells.'

In the end, after constant neglect, many women become addicted to the emptiness of prison life. The alternative on the outside, with all its complexities and hazards, seems a terrifying prospect. Audrey Peckham, a headmistress sent on remand for conspiracy to murder, remembers her feelings of fatalistic security: 'Pucklechurch had become my refuge from the terrors of the outside world, and I hated to leave it. I didn't feel safe. I just wanted to stay inside for ever in a state of suspended animation.' As Chris Tchaikovsky recalls, the prevailing feeling in prison is one of nothingness. 'You don't belong anywhere – lost in a fortress, and often forgotten by those outside.' There are many women inside, she says, and nobody even knows they are there. These are the lost women.

Telecea, the black woman who is such a strong symbol of containment and rebellion in the novel *This Place*, speaks for many lost voices when she pleads to be let out of maximum security and back to the main prison: 'Make them send me back. Back to this place. Think they can take and use me up. Think that metal box can eat my brain. Eat my dreams. Think they can do me so I can't make no more sculptures. So I don't know where I am. I know alright. This place call Max. Been here before. Will be here again. Make them send me back.' Finally, she calls on God as her avenger for her pain and fear and rage: 'Tell me, you; be wherever they be. Lissen and watch. Up in Max or wherever they puts you... Tell me, you be the witness.'

REHABILITATION: TRAINING FOR FREEDOM

Our society exists on the principle of goodies and baddies. But the people in prison are just like everybody else, with good bits and bad bits. (Governor, Holloway)

Psychological approach

Given the common assumption that women who commit crime are in some way 'damaged goods' psychologically, its not surprising that the emphasis on personal therapy is strong in women's prisons. The reality of staff shortages and ill-conceived ideas about what such 'therapy' entails means, however, that treatment, when it is appropriate and available, is not always *adequate*. But there are successful exceptions. June is one. While she was in Holloway, she went to weekly sessions with a psychologist, and began to talk: 'I was just right for it. I was at a time when I wanted to talk about things and get a lot of unhappy memories off my chest. And I jus' didn' care. I'd been hurt so much already. I thought, even if these people knew all these things about me, there's no way I could have been hurt anymore than I'd been hurt already.'

Emma also had good support from a therapist. 'I had a psychologist who I saw regularly, and I could talk to her a lot. It went beyond just being therapy – it was somebody I could let it all out to, and I knew that that was confidential. There was also a social worker that I had a similar relationship with.'

Mary has a rather more jaundiced view of prison psychiatric help. As a long-term drug user, she is regularly hauled up for medical reports. Rarely do they provide any new revelation, or any real support. In an article she wrote about release from prison, Mary says, 'the magistrate, on sentencing me, told me I desperately needed his help, and he would send me to prison for the treatment I so badly required. I would be rehabilitated, given a chance to lead a new, drug-free life. Did he really believe that, or was he just one more liar?' Over the past twenty years, Mary has been sent for hundreds of doctors' reports. None has resulted in anything but temporary heroin-free phases. Mary is consistently told what a messed-up, selfish person she is, and how she should clean up, meet a man, and find true fulfilment that way. As a lesbian, and as a long-term junky, with awareness of what her habit means, and how to control it, Mary is unimpressed.

Anne had a similar experience when she was inside, for knifing her boyfriend whilst out of her brain on a cocktail of alcohol and heroin. The psychiatrist she saw, after doing some cliché-ridden tests with ink blots to 'prove' Freudian fallacies, turned on Anne and applauded the punishment she was being given. 'He told me, "I hope you get a very long sentence, because it's the only way you'll get the guilt out. Five or six years should do it." I said, "I don't deserve that long, because it would have been him or me. Either way it was self defence!"' Coupled with such unwarranted menaces, were the unsolicited attentions of a holy father. Fine, if you're Catholic; not if you're a non-believer. 'I had this stupid priest keep knocking on the door at night – "Come and tell me your sins." I just told him to fuck off.' Psychiatric help *can* be of great use to women who are confused or disturbed in their minds and suffer at their sudden incarceration. But too often the help is either misdirected, or inadequate.

Educational training

Rule One of prison regulations is to assist prisoners to lead a useful life on their release. Holloway governor Colin Allen says wryly, 'One would be less than human if one did not become a bit cynical about that from time to time.' Even where educational facilities are good, and the teaching staff wholly committed – as at Holloway – the strictures of the system, and ever-present staff shortages, prevent consistent results.

Nonetheless, Holloway does offer a very broad base of classes, in a department run by Richard Brown, including English as a foreign language, 'O' and 'A' levels and Open University training, vocational training in things like computer programming and word processing as well as the traditional Home Economics. There are also the creative options of art, pottery, dance and drama. Richard Brown's admirable philosophy works on two levels: one, to enrich prisoners' lives within the stifling environment of prison; and two, to provide them with the opportunity to make choices and changes in their lives – something probably strictly denied them up till now, both inside and outside prison.

Most countries are reluctant to treat the work prisoners do with any kind of respect, so that the gaining of any skill often becomes a mere extension of the punitive programme. Sweden is an honourable exception, according to researcher Cathy Smith, who reported on London Broadcasting Company radio in 1985 that prisoners there were paid full union rates for a forty-hour week, and were allowed home visits twice a month, in preparation for life outside. This new regime was launched in 1972; by 1975 recidivist rates (women offending on a repeated, regular basis) were significantly down.

In Scotland, Emma fought for job training during her sentence, and got it – but found that she was thrown in at the deep end. 'I was actually given a year's "training for freedom", and I worked outside the prison. But there were very few long-sentence women in Scotland. I did that year totally isolated from the rest of the prison. They opened a separate little unit down one end and I had absolutely no contact with other inmates.' She was also given a placement in a local library, which again tested her survival skills. 'They didn't want to talk about prison – and I didn't have anything else to talk about – so it was a case of learning to communicate on a day-to-day level with people who didn't have any knowledge of inside prison and didn't particularly want to have.' Gradually Emma built up a body of experience, which, coupled with academic work for a degree, which she sweated over late at night and early in the morning, since she had no concession from other prison work, stood her in good stead on her release.

June was just as eager to learn. Encouraged by the education officer at Holloway, she applied to the National Extension College (a correspondence course agency) and then Open University. On her release she went straight off to study at a polytechnic. She has nothing but praise for the help she had. 'If I phoned now and said I was feeling depressed, then one of them would come round and say, "Just go home, shut the door, we're comin'." And that's not part of their job.' Always, they keep up hope in the education department, she says, even with the ones who don't make it. 'But they keep thinking, maybe this time it will work. You have to have a good strong core to be able to take knocks like that all the time.'

Oases like this make all the difference for women whose self-confidence has taken a phenomenal knock. In the end, of course, the gulf between prisoners and the rest of the world remains massive. Sonya, art therapist in the novel *This Place*, sums up the inevitable displacement between teacher and pupil, which occurs when the 'school' is a jail house. '"Slow down," she commanded herself silently. "This isn't high school. You don't live here. You can leave at the end of the day. This isn't your real life, it's just a mirage. They're just prisoners. It's not about you."' Just prisoners...

Getting a job

Something which daunts even the most socially privileged – finding employment – is a hurdle of immense proportions for an ex-prisoner. Where do you go? What do you reveal? How do you start? Ann Lindsay remembers the conflicting and useless advice meted out to her: 1) with her (high) qualifications, she'd be OK, whatever; 2) with her (heavy) record she didn't stand a chance in hell, anywhere. She received *no* practical help on coping with interviews, or explaining her past life, and had to negotiate the minefield on her own. She now works for a British organisation, Apex, set up specifically to assist ex-offenders in their search for a job (see chapter 2). Apex helps combat employers' prejudice, which assumes that 'If you commit *one* crime then you'll commit *every* type of crime'. As Ann says: 'When you're a prison inmate nothing you say means anything, and that carries on when you get out.' At the same time, there is an enormous pressure to succeed instantly, as if to 'justify having been given your freedom'.

Women offenders in particular are discriminated against. Apex have trouble persuading prisons and probation officers that they want a job in the first place, and then when they do find a place, they suffer the patronage of ill-informed employers. Says Ann, 'The whole area of women and crime is seen as unnatural: women aren't "naturally" criminal. They're too passive, too acquiescent, they're too caring... So there's a sort of "sickness" about women committing crimes. so employers are more liable to accept, "Oh she was under pressure," etc., because it fits in.' But this concession makes a woman susceptible to all kinds of sexual harassment and blackmail. Ann: 'Once you've got a history of violence or mental instability, you can't respond to things like harassment in the same way that other people could. I'm very conscious of it being easy for people to see you as unstable. Women tend to be classed that way anyway, but if they've got *proof* of it...' This makes the whole ordeal of coming out from behind the wall a hundred per cent more terrifying.

Coming out

Release from prison is rarely the joyful occasion anticipated in those long waiting months inside. The overwhelming feeling of most women is one of pure anti-climax. The struggle starts here. Audrey Peckham, in her book, *A Woman in Custody*, remembers, 'I was glad it was behind me, but I wasn't overcome with joy, or with the sense of freedom, or any such thing. I just plodded down the road, and it seemed such a long road.' For Jacki the feeling was delayed, but the same. 'It hit me after a day. After I'd done the champagne and roses bit, I just came down like a ton of bricks. I went to the doctor for vitamins. He said "Why do you want vitamins?" I said, "I've been in prison, I've not had a good diet." He said, "Well you're not in prison now, I'm going to give you an anti-depressant." I said, "Look I've seen enough of those things," but he refused to give me the vitamins, just gave me a prescription for anti-depressants, which I never used. I thought, "My god, it happens out here as well."'

Release, paradoxically, brings with it strong feelings of isolation. You are now a free woman, back into a world where no-one monitors your movements and few people know what you've been through. Jacki remembers her frustration: 'You start another sentence when you leave. It's the sort of freedom you cannot cope with.' Everything about prison has taught you to do otherwise. Mary writes of her release: 'I know I should be feeling happy, how many friends left behind have said "Wish I was you going out, you've got your freedom at last!" My freedom... Or am I returning to another kind of prison with even more punishment? Prison is easy for some – it's out here the hell starts. I spent so much time lying awake planning for this great day over and over in my mind. How strongly I intended never to use drugs again, how strongly I felt it, not just said it. But I need drugs, now, something... anything just to fill this lonely pain and take away this fear.'

When the initial terror dies down and life begins to be more normal, there always remains a nagging doubt at the back of any ex-prisoner's mind. Emma: 'You know that you're getting on well with people – they seem to like you – but underneath you know that there's a very big part of you that they know nothing at all about.' So who do you tell, and how do you tell it? Women badly need advice on these sorts of social dilemmas – but they learn to be wary of seeking help from officialdom because they know that these state organisations have been 'taught to treat prisoners with no respect'. The social stigma is a constant burden. Says Jacki, 'I imagine for the rest of my life, if I ever achieve anything, the papers will dig this up – "ex-blackmailer" – I'll have this following me around forever.'

Often the best encouragement comes from self-help groups, where a common knowledge and a shared past take away that lurking fear of rejection and encourage a more creative use of life outside. In

London, Clean Break Theatre, and the Creative and Supportive Trust, as well as Women in Prison (see chapter 2), offer advice specifically for women offenders. They are badly needed.

Otherwise, the outlook is bleak. The most fundamental needs – like housing – are rarely provided. Mary: 'Even for the women who ask (in prison) it's very rare that they'll get them a flat or anywhere to live. They might get you into a women's hostel, but then women like me they won't take, because of drugs.' The bitter word on the tip of everyone's tongue is – failure. June talks about friends she knew inside: 'I have a friend – God, she was comin' out to do all these wonderful things, and she stuck it for a little while. Went to college and did really well, and then jus' couldn' handle it any more. And I think that happens so many times. And a lot of women – you see them in there, in their late twenties, and they're still children.'

Even profoundly capable women, like Agnes, find it so demoralising to adapt: 'When they let you out that gate, you're happy because you're out, but then you think, "Shit, what do I do now?" You try for a job, nobody wants to know. You try for a house, nobody wants to know. You try for a council flat, nobody wants to know. I finished up, on comin' out of prison, living in the battered wives' home for twelve months before I got this poxy thing. It's like a fucking rabbit hutch. I call it Cookham Wood!' Agnes is bitter. And seven years after her release, Jacki, as many women like her, is still mystified at her experience, 'still trying to salvage something from it, make it mean something'. Still sore, and angry.

FIGHT BACK: USING THE SYSTEM

> It may well be as the end of the century draws nearer, penological progress will result in even fewer or no women at all being given prison sentences. (Official Home Office statement)

> Oh, for a magician's wand, a riot, the revolution, to set the victim free and put the greyhound there. (*Victims and Victors*, Don Tomson, Pluto, 1985)

From the venerable art of splitting matches, to the tortuous bureaucracy of applying for parole, there are an infinite number of loopholes and stumbling blocks in prison life, which you must learn to negotiate – or else suffer. There is no way of winning head-on against the state machine in its most oppressive punitive stance, but there are ways of oiling that machine so that it runs a little more smoothly for you – or, if necessary – putting a medium-sized spanner in the works. One thing each ex-prisoner I spoke to stressed: if there is something you want, you must fight, wheedle, or cheat the authorities till you get it. This is a point of honour.

Sometimes playing the system is a form of collusion with authority, something recognised as 'right wing' behaviour among sister prisoners. And Jacki realised, halfway through her sentence that 'I had always been doffing a cap to the system'. In her case this was a kind of middle-class obedience – but something she learned to turn subtly on its head. As usual, class was in her favour. 'It's like there are two prisons really: one for certain types of offenders who buck the system and get beaten, and prison for people like me – weedy, middle-class – who are afraid to say boo to a goose.' Even when she did start saying 'boo', she wangled a cushy number – the coveted gardens job. 'Mostly middle-class people went to the gardens. I then got in with the arty clique – you know, read the *Sunday Times*, eat quiche, get garlic in on their wages.' These were the politely naughty creatures who made 'ingenious concoctions with cornflakes and cocoa powder' for birthday parties. For all the world like a girls' dorm. But it helped pass the time: an essential aim for any prisoner.

Black or poor women have less background privileges to draw on for their survival, but still there are ways and means. June, a Jamaican woman, explains: 'It's a weird system. You can't beat it but you can work it. It's just as well that I've got a quick brain – that I learned to work it my own way.' For June, the key need was education. So she went all out to get her Open University training. It was hard work – getting the necessary books, and seeing her tutor regularly – but she buttered up the prison officers, even the ones she hated – 'If they were ever to have looked in my eyes they would have known' – and the things she needed were duly supplied. (There are networks of support open to women inside and outside prison (see chapter 2) – but you need to know where they are, and how to use them.)

Emma recognises this need for careful coercion: 'it does in fact make you very manipulative, because it's the only way you can actually achieve anything. You do get very good at playing the system. But then they know that's what you're doing.' She had particularly vivid memories of the manoeuvres necessary to get an early release date: 'If you know that the only way you can get out is through the parole systems, you soon behave to what you think the parole board is going to want.' Which of course means playing the little lady... 'The first thing you learn is that there is absolutely no way that you can be aggressive or violent.' She managed her parole in the end, and also struggled for full educational facilities. She is ironic about this: 'I'm often held up as a quite good example of what prison can do. I'm actually much more of an example of what can happen *despite* the system. Because the system at no point helped me. I did a lot of studying in prison, but I had to fight for it. And for the first three years of that study I was actually told, "If you want to do this, it's in your own time. And you must perform all the normal prison duties as we expect them to be done." And I actually got my degree by waking up at one every morning and studying till six. And doing my normal prison day from six am till eight o'clock at night... I bloody well had to do it the hard way. They were *not* making it easy for me – I had to bargain for what I got.'

Bitter sweet memories flood through, of times spent wangling your way around a crazy prison regime. Chris Tchaikovsky served garden duty during her time in Holloway. She has fond recollections of the goat she trained to butt prison officers' behinds... and is still reeling from the time she turned to a bare patch of earth and started to dig it over lovingly, with thoughts of potato and spring cabbage. Halfway through her endeavour she was hollered at from the window: 'Stop, stop – that was Ruth Ellis's burial ground!' The last woman to be hanged in Britain: no cross, no sign at all. About to be turned into early veg. Was this a wind-up from the prison officer, or the truth? Life inside is strange.

One thing prison fosters very quickly is a self-awareness rarely gained in the more comfortable outside world. Some women do not learn, and come back and back to jail, without taking new knowledge away with them. But many end up not only bruised but also brighter, with an acute perception of what it is all about. June believes that prison made her grow up. 'As an only child I think I was very controlled by my parents. I came to England, got married, and gave someone *else* the responsibility – and actually that was why I got nicked. Because he died and I was left, responsible for me, and I didn't know what the fuck to do. So I just went to pieces.' Once inside, however, 'I grew up. First of all I discovered in prison that I was responsible for *me*, for my own actions.' But the praise for this goes to her, and not the institution: 'I think I was one of the rare, rare cases where prison worked. It was what I needed. But then *I* did it, the prison didn't do it.'

Somehow, June, and others like her, learned to draw on inner resources they had never recognised in themselves before. 'I was seen as having a kind of inner strength – and that's because I was sorting myself out. I was growing up, I was dealing with a whole lot of things very quickly.' As Chris Tchaikovsky told me, while inside you have loads of time to think about things. You learn to be resilient, to survive and surface again. As she remarked, the woman who comes in and cries is comforted for the first few days. After that she is reprimanded by the other prisoners: this is not the time nor place for wallowing in emotion. It could kill you.

Despite the apparent brusqueness of such behaviour, the camaraderie among women in prison is strong and fertile. Mandy was alone out of all the ex-prisoners I spoke to in saying that she never made any strong bonds during her sentence. Marianne's *only* network of friends were those who'd shared her lifetime of remand and institutionalisation: 'I met some real good friends in prison, plus a few that I'd been in care with.' And Emma remembers that 'although the whole experience of prison is absolutely dreadful, you are accustomed to the company of women. You have a common bond with those women.'

Jacki took a while to adjust to her new environment, but slowly realised: 'I *do* wanna know these people – they're more exciting, they *are* different to other people, there's more life to them. They are kinder, more alive. They are more adventurous and daring and defiant... And I began to really like women. I hadn't really related to women properly before. I'd always had a slight barrier there, and now I thought – I really like women. I even fancy one or two of them.'

For Jenny, too, prison was a revelation. As a business woman she had been used to exploiting people for profit, but now, 'For the first time I lived with women only, and without that materialistic rat race. There were no pressures. We were all equal.'

There's no sense in getting romantic – prison is cruel and heartless. The good things it does breed are due to the survival mechanisms of the human spirit rather than any innate qualities within the system. The gentle rebellion women employ to use the system is a small, subversive protest against something designed to dehumanise and humiliate them. For a woman to stop knitting and start a theatre group (Clean Break Theatre); for a woman to come out of prison and not forget those she leaves behind, but start a campaigning group specifically to help them (Women in Prison); for women to speak up about their times inside – on television and in books like these; for these things to happen, is a minor miracle. Telecea in *This Place* was labelled a dangerous psychopath – but then she started to sculpt and paint. She is not a fiction, but a symbol of thousands of women who, in the middle of abject isolation of body and mind, hear a small voice inside saying, 'I got power, you know I got me some power, and I say this head ain't never gonna hurt no more. Never no more.'[8]

The strongest willpower in the world cannot always shake off predetermined convictions, however. Should a woman fight to be different, or should she not fit the conventional image of femininity, there are ways of containing her power, other than imprisonment or criminalisation. There is another label, more complex and dangerous than 'bad', more damaging in its restrictions, more wide-ranging in its implications. It is a label familiar to women, from the witches of the middle ages to the rebels of the twentieth century. Not 'bad'? Then definitely '*mad*'.

CHAPTER 4

MADNESS AND CRIME: THE DOOMED SEARCH FOR POTENCY

Imagine *me* a psychopath. I've read about them in the papers.
(June, 'The Silent Twins', BBC, January 1986)

There are bits in everyone that are furious and frustrated and hurt.
(Psychologist Maggie Hilton)

'You can be mad at the world', said Bea, 'but you still can't make
it do what you want it to.' (*The Madness of a Seduced Woman*, Susan
Fromberg Schaeffer, Pan, 1985)

Madness is really 'a doomed search for potency'. (Phyllis Chesler,
Women and Madness, Avon, 1972)

'MANMADE' MADNESS: A HISTORY

Madness is a strange, shifting, emotive concept. It is used both as a term of personal abuse – a way of discrediting someone who breaks the boundaries of acceptable social behaviour – and as a grander metaphor for the general chaos of human life. Madness is anything too big for us to take.

Madness is also a concept often used in criminology. 'Not bad but mad' is a tediously trite little phrase trotted out repeatedly to describe behaviour which seems to evade the more 'rational' areas of crime, and head for murkier depths of emotionally-inspired deviance. 'Mad' is a derogatory term here. It implies a lack of control, a failure in the face of everyday demands. Criminal acts are already a threat to the status quo. If these acts cannot be thoroughly justified in a logical manner, by courts, juries, newspapers and public, then the threat they pose is magnified. 'Mad' is a safe adjective for such manifestly dangerous behaviour.

Women are often assumed to be more inclined to 'sick' or 'mad' behaviour than men. This is an irrational belief which yawns back to the birth of Christianity, and the concurrent challenge to female power and status. We still have not shaken that belief off. It is a thoroughly effective means of ignoring female strength. In 1970 Dr I. K. Broverman conducted a psychological study to examine people's ideas of what constituted a healthy person. Independence, and all other related qualities, were seen as desirable in a man – and were also believed to constitute a healthy adult. But these same 'healthy' attributes in a woman were seen as undesirable and unattractive. The participants' ideal woman would be 'emotional', 'submissive', 'dependent'. But she would not, it appears, be *healthy*. Sickness in women is the expected norm.[1]

Following on, like a macabre self-fulfilling prophecy, is the undeniable fact that far more women than men end up being committed to psychiatric hospitals at some point in their lives. Looking at the figures for prison, and the figures for hospital, a dramatic reversal takes place. In 1981 2,200 women were admitted to prison in Britain for custody, as opposed to 40,000 men. In the same year, 74,963 men landed up in psychiatric institutions – but so did 110,551 women.[2] As Phyllis Chesler remarks in her book *Women and Madness*, all the *clinical* studies of insanity rely on women, and all the *criminal* studies on men. Literature reinforces the accepted pattern – and the prejudice. It is deeply ingrained in western society that men, when distressed, will lash out, punishing others for their frustrations, while women hold it all in, mutilating *themselves*, physically and mentally, rather than put the blame on someone else. And even when men, too, become psychologically disturbed they are the ones who tend to violence against others, while women turn more easily to self-destruction.[3] In Deborah Spungen's tragic modern story of punk musician Sid Vicious, and his doomed affair with her daughter Nancy, she recognises that 'Both were troubled and angry. Sid had the capacity to lash out in anger at others. Nancy tended to direct her anger at herself.'[4] In the end it was Sid who stabbed Nancy with a kitchen knife before killing himself: two children of a 'No Future' generation, acting out deadly patterns from an ancient past.

If women are thought to verge constantly on the crazy anyway, then women who deviate enough from the norm to commit any sort of crime – always a male province – are doubly vulnerable to damaging labels, whether mental illness is cited in the case or not. And indeed, says Emma, 'There are many assumptions about why women commit crimes' – she has personally suffered from many of them, after her long spell in prison – 'and they're *all* emotional or mental.' This assumption of female sickness in crime goes back to theories of biological determinism – a throwback to the nineteenth century, which has lingered well into this one, and which is applied to criminal *and* non-criminal women. Says ex-prisoner Jenny Hicks, 'A man isn't seen as getting depressed because of his biology' – a 'logical' reason is sought instead. In the history of female crime and insanity, and its treatment, logic like this seems to play no part.

Before the Age of Reason, the 'fool' or the 'village idiot' was embraced within the medieval community, although treated pretty roughly. *He* may even have been seen as a wise prophet – though *she* was often condemned as a witch. With the approach of a neater mechanical age, society started to favour incarceration: the cordoning off of scapegoats. So when the infamous Bedlam hostel was opened in

London in the sixteenth century, it was not just the insane, but also the poor, delinquent and inadequate who were flung inside. Definitions of crime, illness and moral responsibility were still to be forged. As the years went by, separate corners for prisons and psychiatric hospitals emerged, and although humane attitudes were encouraged by people like the Quakers, with their plea for 'caring custody', by the nineteenth century psychiatric institutions were still fearsomely grim places, with firmly locked doors, and a regime of ice-cold showers and the regular application of leeches, to suck out the badness in people's souls...

It was in the harshly moral Victorian era that theories about women 'deviants' emerged – echoes of which reverberate, damagingly, to this day. Lombroso and Ferrero, two Italian criminologists, published a work called *The Female Offender* (Fisher Unwin, 1895) in which they used the conventions of the day (measuring craniums to 'prove' atavistic tendencies in law breakers) to launch a virulent attack on women criminals – and on women as a sex. This was hailed as a seminal work.

By attacking a fact of life – female *biology* – the two 'scientists' made their argument hard to refute. Although it seems blatant and ridiculous now to affirm that women do not 'naturally' commit crime, because, to quote Lombroso, of 'a conservatism of which the primary cause is to be sought in the immobility of the ovule compared with zoosperm', and that therefore when they *do* break laws 'we may conclude that (their) wickedness must have been enormous', in the nineteenth century this pseudo-rationalism was absorbed immediately into the bloodstream of legal and social attitudes towards women and crime.

All the ancient fears of women rear up here in cogent form. Women who deviate are ugly and repellent, says Lombroso. They even have *wrinkles*: 'In this connection we may recall the proverbial wrinkles of witches...' And while 'normal' women are 'organically conservative', black women like 'Red Indians' and 'Negresses' are positively masculine and 'savage'. The criminal woman, meanwhile, is simply 'a monster'.

Do these vicious views about race and sex seem preposterous in our more enlightened century? Even if they do, they form a bedrock for current attitudes about women. *All* criminal and emotional problems among women are inherently based on biology, says Lombroso. Insanity in women is 'hysteria' – a disturbance of the womb. And in the 'female criminal lunatics' he studied, he reckoned that 'their madness becomes more acute at particular periods, such as menstruation, menopause and pregnancy.' Normal female biological functions were now beginning to be seen as illnesses in themselves (and in the 1980s the debate about 'premenstrual syndrome' rages still. See this chapter, 'women breaking down'). We carry the legacy of Lombroso and Ferrero around still. They have yet to be refuted.

By the beginning of the twentieth century, simple notions of custody of disturbed patients were replaced by different ideas about treatment and cure. New theories involving psychoanalysis were illuminating in their serious assessment of the human mind, but were nonetheless sometimes misused on women. In the wrong hands psychoanalysis, a potential tool for liberation, became a new means of repression. Medical means of controlling mental illness, including insulin treatment, electro-convulsive therapy and psychosurgery, were also introduced.

By the 1940s and 1950s new approaches led to an 'open door' policy on mental health, the old locked door regimes being replaced by occupational therapy, community care, and the prescriptions of psychotropic (mood-altering) drugs. This apparent leniency brought its own problems. Not only did we now have generations of women addicted to valium – the idea of women being seen as 'naturally' disturbed still permeates many a doctor's prescription pad – but, as psychologist Maggie Hilton explains, some women started committing crime as an act of desperation, through a lack of monitoring by the new, mental health approach – 'people get criminalised because there's lack of care in psychiatric hospitals.'

In the 1970s it became clear, in Britain at least, that there was a huge gap between psychiatric hospitals and the very severe 'special hospitals' reserved for the 'criminally insane'. There was nowhere for the non-violent mentally ill offender to go. With this realisation came the idea for 'secure units' – halfway houses between prison and hospital, an idea not yet fully realised due to lack of funding. Meanwhile, inside prison the emphasis was, as ever, female instability. Male prisons retained their mainly punitive approach, while Holloway made special provision not only for its small number of mentally ill women prisoners – but for *all* the inmates, by completely redesigning the interior along psychiatric lines. John Camp, writing in the mid-1970s, affirmed that 'conventional prisons are unnecessary for the vast majority of women. Their offences are due mainly to personality disorders, which will respond to psychiatric treatment'.[5] From 'sick bodies' to 'sick minds' – the legacy of Lombroso came home to roost. Much of the treatment of women offenders, and of women who are deemed mentally ill, is still based on male fear and ignorance. Shut her in, shut her up, is the safest line to take for prison officers and for doctors, and, as one woman put it in *Women and the Psychiatric Paradox* 'I feel that, essentially, when a doctor prescribes a pill for me, it's to put *him* out of *my* misery.'[6]

There is no reason to suppose that contemporary methods of dealing with distressed women are that much more effective or understanding than those of the Middle Ages. The labels applied to them are arbitrary, their treatment often far removed from personal needs. As psychiatric social worker, Valerie, says, 'The line between mad and bad is so fine – and when you're actually in the system you become aware that what the person has done and who they are, and what is going on in their life, is the least relevant issue.'

Modern woman is under severe strain to be all things to all people, and, as one woman suggested to me, 'women may commit crimes because of the mental distress caused by women's lack of identity in advanced capitalist countries, and isolation in the nuclear family'. Author Carol Smart also finds it quite conceivable that it is the 'untenable nature of the traditional feminine role in the first place that produces a high incidence of breakdown among women.'[7]

'Madness' has its own politics. The causes can be social as much as personal, as Roger Smith points out in his paper on 'Medicine and murderous women'. As psychiatry developed in the nineteenth century, he writes, it formed the basis for humane judgements (as well as erroneous *value* judgements). Thus women who killed their newborn babies were not charged with murder, but with a new term – 'infanticide'. This was a label linked to biology, since it linked the killing of a baby with its mother's physical and mental state following childbirth, and although humane indeed, in that it stopped many women going to the gallows, it ignored the fact that 'the most widespread form of baby murder occurred in relation to illegitimate births'. The strain and stigma of pregnancy outside marriage was a valid enough reason for desperate action, as much as the purely biological response of 'puerperal mania'.[8]

Social expectations of womanhood generally still prevail over any consideration of the individual. As Emma says of the attitude inside prison: 'It doesn't matter if you're depressed and have got problems, just be passive and obedient, and some day you'll make a man a good wife.' On the other hand, if you rebel against the norm, you may end up labelled insane, like the wilful ill-fated heroine of *The Madness of a Seduced Woman* (Pan, 1983), who shot another woman in thwarted passion and jealousy. She was someone 'too big' for people to take: 'Everyone said I was born restless and too sensitive and intelligent for my own good. And I was relentlessly curious.' The reward for her particular rebellion was rejection by a man much 'smaller' than herself; a desperate crime in retaliation for his lack of love; and a life-long committal to psychiatric hospital. All payment for the fact that 'All I ever wanted to do was invent a new world – and of course I failed.'

WOMEN BREAKING DOWN

'When I was three my father fractured my skull, and then I had my skull fractured over and over throughout my adult life.' (Annette)

'...the streamlined insanity of their behaviour was the product, in the beginning, of crude longing dug out from their heart.' (Janet Frame, *Faces in the Water*, Women's Press, 1980)

Too much to bear

Psychologist Maggie Hilton regularly faces women in her work who have broken down under the pressure of their daily lives – and may well, in addition, have committed crimes of varying severity. When looking for the reasons behind their actions she often has to dig right back to their early years. A breakdown sows seeds early, and germinates long. 'These women', she says, 'have often had violence done to them in childhood, and later.' The pattern of self-destruction is set when they are only girls – teaching them to strike at their own hearts, since it is there that the people they love seem to be aiming anyway.

The women I spoke to who suffered some psychiatric disturbance had all learned to fundamentally despise themselves, either as dependent, needy, 'weak' people – all the things women are supposed to be, and yet are punished for; or for being something doubly threatening to white, western society – black, for instance, or lesbian: any category outside the suburban norm. Candy's problems started very early, with her 'mother's obvious dislike' of her. At fifteen, this led to 'constant absconding' from home, because 'I had thought it would make me happier, and that my mother would show she cared and have me home again – although this was not the case.' Running away led to petty arson, and eventually landed her in Broadmoor: 'I was nineteen and in a nuthouse, but I felt about fifteen – all I wanted was my mum, and she was nowhere near.'

A Polish woman whom psychiatric social worker Valerie saw as a client was suffering intensely, because her husband – with whom she had had a long and dependent relationship – had recently died. 'She became more and more profoundly depressed – she started feeling that she really was a bad person and shouldn't be alive. She hadn't got many friends, but she started to feel that her closest friend, an elderly woman, reflected all the things she wasn't – that her friend was a better person – and she decided that both of them should be dead.'

She knifed and severely wounded the other woman, and then tried to kill herself. The treatment she received was woefully inadequate.

She spent four months in Holloway, where her difficulties with the language, and the increasing realisation of what she had done, led her into an even deeper depression. Finally she was sent to a psychiatric hospital, where the psychiatrists wanted to give her electro-convulsive therapy. Valerie was appalled at this lack of sensitivity: 'You want to stick bloody electrical charges in her to make *you* feel better', but she is herself pessimistic about the alternatives. This woman, already low in self-esteem, is now riddled with guilt: 'She *wants* to be punished'. The pattern of self-loathing, once so firmly set, is practically impossible to break.

Women often break down in the face of restrictive social attitudes, suffering personal privations for the community's failing. A middle-class Pakistani woman started shoplifting, although she had no material need to, and was seen by psychologist Maggie Hilton, who discovered that the woman's husband was having an affair. The strain of holding in her feelings about this – and with her cultural background, 'you do not talk about your husband's faults' – led to attention-seeking behaviour. The same was true for one of social worker Patricia C's clients, a middle-class woman with a cleanliness fetish, who was unusually dependent on her parents, and had threatened them both with violence. Patricia C believed her to have lesbian feelings, which, in her restricted social sphere, were taboo.

Other social prejudices such as racism also lead to unreasonable punishment. A colleague explains: 'I remember a close friend who was busted at the age of eleven in her school. She was carrying cannabis. She was naive – and the teacher saw it and took her out of the classroom. The girl was taken down to the police station and given a stripsearch. She ended up in a mental home. She was black.' Condemning black women to madness is a way of defusing their threat, as writer Jean Rhys shows in her book, *Wide Sargasso Sea*. We all know the moving story of Mr Rochester, who is burdened with a 'mad' wife and therefore not free to marry the lovely, white, gracious Jane Eyre. What we do *not* know from Charlotte Brontë's book is the fictitious history of the first Mrs Rochester – described by Jean Rhys as a beautiful Creole woman who is literally condemned to madness by her husband, after he hears of her mother's insanity. His fear of hereditary lunacy – and perhaps his fear of her black and potent beauty itself – leads him to drive *her* mad.

Phyllis Chesler, in her brilliant work *Women and Madness*, describes madness as 'a cry of powerlessness which is mercilessly punished.' Underneath that impotence lies a towering rage – one that is rarely allowed out, but remorselessly directed inward. Fifty per cent of the women who see psychologist Maggie Hilton start to express anger in their therapy sessions, but, as Phyllis Chesler remarks, 'Anger is a painful and dangerous display for those who feel and are relatively powerless.' For that reason, the fury at untenable situations is contained within, or is turned to more acceptable female emotions – such as guilt and self-loathing.

Annette suffered so many setbacks in her life – from being battered as a child, to seeing her invalid mother die, to a bad marriage and the death of her child, that she assumed it was all her own fault. She was bad, she must be punished – the only place which was fit for her was a hospital for the 'criminally insane': Broadmoor. Under pressure in her job, Annette started a small fire in her workplace, knowing it would be discovered within minutes of its starting, and believing, in her distress, that this was the only way she could escape the building, and thereby also escape her intolerable work burden. Even though the police recognised that this was a one-off case of minor arson, Annette persuaded her solicitor that she was 'bad' enough for Broadmoor. Her prophecy was self-fulfilling, and she spent several miserable years inside.

Candy, an absconder, and later an arsonist, recalls similar emotions. Her frustration turned inexorably to self-mutilation: 'In 1973, in my distress at being an unloved child and unable to understand my torn emotions, I was turning my anger inwards towards myself. Self-mutilation became frequent and I was placed in psychiatric hospital for treatment. However, after one morning they could find nothing mentally wrong with me. Just attention-seeking.' How many years of pent-up emotion and despair go to fill that one small word: 'Just'?

Blame her biology

Lombroso's biological determinism, in his pioneering study of women and crime, set the trend for many theories about the 'madness' inherent in the female body. British doctor Henry Maudsley was 'one of the first British doctors to identify the normal functionings of women's bodies as a cause of insanity and deviance', arguing that normal menstruation, pregnancy and lactation could form part of a pathological condition. Taking this materialist view of behaviour to its limits, he concluded that sexual 'deviations' in women were attributable to the '...irritation of the ovaries or uterus – a disease by which the chaste and modest woman is transformed into a raging fury of lust'.

The menstruating woman has always inspired fear and incomprehension among men. Originally the source of her power (because it indicates her capacity to produce children) the monthly flow of blood has been turned into a secret, shameful bodily function which must be kept as invisible as possible, to the extent of wearing internal tampons, and even using absurd and dangerous vaginal sprays to mask any natural smells. Not surprisingly, menstruation has moved from being a time for quiet contemplation and increased bodily receptivity to an irritant, a source of pain and discomfort. Premenstrual tension has become an all-pervasive modern complaint. Lombroso reckoned that in the female 'criminal lunatic', 'her madness becomes more acute at particular periods such as menstruation, menopause and pregnancy'. Spanning the centuries to the present day and still in the 1980s women's magazines are full of articles about how to combat PMT. It is in this decade too that a more extreme and controversial 'illness' has become topical again: premenstrual *syndrome* (PMS).

In Britain, Dr Katharina Dalton is the foremost proponent of the PMS argument. PMS, she says, is a syndrome which occurs just *before* menstruation, due to an extreme deficiency in the hormone progesterone. While women with premenstrual tension may feel irritable and moody, sufferers of PMS may also experience strong psychological disturbances, as well as physical symptoms like asthma, migraine and sinusitis. Says Dr Dalton: 'Something like forty per cent of women suffer some sort of symptom each month. Only about ten per cent of them need treatment or deserve treatment. And out of those there's about one in 10,000 where their hormone imbalance is responsible for crime.' Dr Dalton has appeared in court on behalf of several women – some of them, like Christine English, up on murder charges – for whom the defence of PMS has provided a more lenient sentence, or complete discharge.[10] Her treatment for PMS, sometimes a condition of liberty for those she has defended, constitutes large doses of progesterone. There is, says Dr Dalton, a blood test for PMS (although it has limited application) in which the sex hormone binding globulin, is low in sufferers. Increased progesterone raises it.

Precise details are needed about a woman's cycle, and her crime, for PMS to be a plausible defence – and in the few cases where it is used successfully, the physical facts seem to be conclusive. But, of course, this is a dangerous area. As Corinne Squire wrote in British magazine *The Leveller* (December 1981), the popular press use distorted definitions of PMS to make sweeping statements about women in general. In 1981, after the Christine English case, the *Daily Mirror* screamed, 'at certain times of the month, and for no other reason, some women can go berserk'. As Corinne Squire says of PMT *and* PMS, '(This) is partly a fulfilment of the meanings that men have constructed for women; it demonstrates an instability and stupidity in women that absolves men from fear in the fact of menstruation.' The manipulation of female 'frailty' is hardly warranted, if we remember that, while some women commit nasty crimes at certain times of the month, many more men commit far nastier crimes at *all* times. Are we to gather from this that men's hormonal responses are even more volatile and unpredictable than those of women?

The crime of infanticide is also linked with female biology and psychology. In the case of Martha Brixey in 1845, Roger Smith unearths an early contender for PMS. He quotes contemporary reports: 'The prisoner, a quiet, inoffensive girl, a maidservant in a respectable family, was charged with the murder of an infant. She had laboured under disordered menstruation and, a short time before the occurrence, had shown some violence of temper about trivial domestic matters.' She cut the throat of her charge, a small child – and then immediately told her master. She was acquitted 'on the ground of insanity, probably arising from obstructed menstruation.' Roger Smith's accompanying remarks are interesting. 'Her and the public, if proper provision was made for her, need have no further worries. her violence was accordingly a matter between her and society's delegated specialists.'[11] (The specialists are usually white, middle-class, middle-aged men: not representative of all society's members, by any means.)

As Deborah Spungen's gruelling account of her drug addict daughter's desperate life reveals, the failure is not so much that of the individual – in this case Nancy – but of the rest of the community. 'One doctor they saw about Nancy said, "She's vulnerable. She was overmedicated as a child, and society has failed to provide the means to ease her pain".' It was easier for society to condemn her as a social failure, and leave her to her own personal despair: '"She hates being alive," I said. "She hates her pain. She hates herself. She wants to destroy herself."' And after the sordid killing of her daughter, Deborah writes: 'Nancy's death was dignified in my fantasy. In death, she had at last found the peace she never found in life...It did not work out that way. A murderer intervened. Nancy died under a hotel sink with a knife in her stomach, the whole world there to gape at her. She died the subject of ridicule and scorn. The press called her Nauseating Nancy...They made it seem like she got what she deserved...Nobody wanted to hear of her pain, her sadness, her sensitivity. Nobody wanted to understand Nancy. Nobody cared.'[12]

Treatment or punishment?

Just as there is a fine line between being labelled 'mad' or 'bad', there is also confusion in Britain about appropriate treatment for the offender who is thought to be mentally ill. Psychiatric social worker Valerie says it is pure 'chance' whether one of her clients ends up in prison or hospital. When someone is arrested and the police are called, she says 'At that point somebody may say – in the case of women more often – she's acting strange. In fact she's probably showing, 99 per cent of the time, a normal reaction to suddenly being dragged away for some minor deviancy, to wherever it is – C1, the psychiatric unit of Holloway. She'll be seen by the Holloway psychiatrist who, if he decides that she seems a bit "mad", will immediately be thinking of that wonderful word – "disposal".'

Whether she is 'disposed of' in hospital or not can often depend on something as mundane as the level of admission rates in a particular area. It is that arbitrary. And as usual, it is men who quickly learn to manipulate the system to their own advantage. When someone offends and is thought to be mentally ill, they can be put under a 'section', which means they can be held for up to 28 days for medical assessment, under the 1983 British Mental Health Act, or for up to six months (it is then reviewable by doctors) in psychiatric hospital – as opposed to a fixed prison sentence imposed by the courts. Men who regularly offend in a minor way, says Valerie, sometimes learn to 'act mad'. Then they are sent to hospital, not prison – and after behaving well for a couple of weeks, they are released. 'I don't know of one woman in my experience', she says, 'who has done this.'

Since psychiatric hospitals have ceased to be locked institutions, prison is being used increasingly, as Pat Carlen reports in *Women's Imprisonment*, as 'a depository for the most difficult people who cannot be treated anywhere else – certainly not in mental hospitals, with their open door policy'. Prisons assume a degree of maladjustment in their inmates anyway – and in the USA as well as Britain, new approaches to the 'mentally disturbed' prisoner have evolved throughout the 1970s. Virginia Pendergrass, writing in *The Female Offender* (ed. Annette Brodsky, Sage Publications, USA, 1975), refers to the introduction of behaviour modification (i.e. if someone behaves 'well', she is encouraged and rewarded), transactional analysis and other forms of modern therapy. There is, however, the perennial problem, she says, a lack of money to see these programmes through – and the problem of reliance on volunteers, who may not always have sufficient expertise. More basic a problem is the paradox that prison means punishment, and hospital treatment. Surely the two are mutually exclusive, not interchangeable?

Whatever the theories or good intentions, disturbed women offenders often end up, initially at least, in a prison cell. Their reception, at places like Holloway, is not always adequate, to say the least. *Nursing Times* (August 28, 1985) reported that 'many doctors see the major aim of the reception consultation as being to sift out the suicidal from the non-suicidal and the troublesome from the more peaceful.' After this cursory consideration, and with a later examination by two doctors, to file a court report on the inmate's mental health, the acute cases are sent to the psychiatric wing, C1 Block, Holloway. This badly lit, grim prison block, described by Dr John Wilkins on British television as 'quite the worst kind of environment you could put women like this into' ('The London Programme', ITV, June 28, 1985), has consistently been criticised in the media, and by prison workers and inmates, as hopelessly inadequate. Jean, a former inmate on C1, recalls her distress: 'I'd just shout and roar at the bare wall. It was the isolation. I just went out of my head completely.' Anne, another ex-inmate, remembers someone in the next cell being driven mad with frustration: 'All night she was banging her head against the wall and no-one came in to stop her. By the time morning came there was half her scalp all over the wall.'

One thing done to appease such suffering is to administer a high dosage of psychotropic drugs. This, too, is a subject of deep controversy, since not only those in obvious distress are given sedatives, but the rest of the female prison population too. Women, deemed more disruptive than men, are drugged heavily to subdue difficult behaviour. Research carried out by Radical Alternatives to Prison in 1979, revealed that 514 doses per woman per year of psychotropic drugs were administered in Holloway. In Pentonville, a male prison, only 37 doses were given out. *World Medicine* expressed its concern in an editorial (October 30, 1982) which stated that, 'This is almost Gulag territory: there are men and women in our prisons who are receiving what amounts to punitive medicine, something most people identify with Siberia. As the British Medical Association well knows from first-hand evidence, potentially dangerous psychotropic drugs are often prescribed, sometimes on a monstrous scale.' Emma certainly remembers being 'skewed out of my brain' on tranquillisers, not only in prison but during her trial as well (see Chapter 3, p. 51). 'All it does', she says, 'is distance you from the problem.' In no way does it tackle the *causes*, or offer a *solution* to what has gone wrong.

Not only do the prisons fail to alleviate women's misery adequately, they even expect a high level of suffering, including self-inflicted wounds. Says social worker Patricia C. 'The attitude towards the women in prison is that it's normal to cut up.' Moreover other inmates are expected to cope with each other's distress. One woman in Styal prison had to sit for hours with someone who had cut herself and was pouring blood (see Chapter 3).

The lack of sensitivity to women in psychological danger in prison is revealed in Anne's story of her arrest and incarceration. In a state of shock after knifing someone and suffering from heroin withdrawal, Anne was nonetheless left on her own entirely when she first entered Holloway. 'Because of what I'd done they thought I might be a psychopathic maniac or something, so they locked me in this little cubicle for two hours – and by the end of it I'd managed to wrap a belt round my neck, and was just about to hang, when someone caught me.' After this she was locked in a cell with 'all sorts of disturbed people', including one woman who 'started running at the wall and banging her head against it'. Neither move – enforced isolation or close proximity to other disturbed women, was likely to calm her down.

The ignorance of some prison officers about mental illness leads to many potential and actual tragedies. When Emma was in prison (see Chapter 3) she was stopped from seeing her psychologist, and was on the verge of a nervous breakdown because of it, when a psychiatrist intervened and had her sessions restarted. The breakdown was avoided.

Sarah Hewer was not so lucky. She was in Pucklechurch remand centre, and was a known epileptic with severe behavioural problems. Because of this she was put in the hospital wing, but as *Nursing Times* reports (August 28, 1985) she was nonetheless given inadequate care. At 2am one night she asked to be let out of her cell because of breathing difficulties. This was refused. Later the next morning she was turned away from the doctor and given instead a major tranquilliser. At 11.45am she suffered a cardiac arrest and died. At her inquest the senior medical officer said that Sarah's 'extreme emotional state' could have brought on acute heart failure. Was the care of Sarah adequate? Should she have been in a remand prison at all, given her difficult psychological state? Whatever the implications, it's too late for Sarah.

Despite such stories, many women would prefer to be in prison to the alternative – psychiatric hospital or 'special hospital', specifically for the violent and mentally ill offender. If anything, these places enjoy an even worse reputation than ordinary prisons. And unlike prison, where you have a fixed sentence, in special hospital you can be held 'without limit of time' – until the institution deems you fit to be let loose.

Mary, a long-term junky and prostitute, got used to her drug addiction being seen solely as a mental illness. Ever since school days, when she was admitted to a psychiatric hospital for absconding (she then also absconded from hospital too, 'I just buggered off') she has resisted psychiatric labels. She knows why she takes drugs – to blank off the pain of her own particular circumstances, and she is a prostitute simply to support her habit. In her time she has been sectioned, and submitted to electric shock treatment and often 'it was a real fight to get put in prison. I really wanted to go to prison rather than go back there'. Emma, too, had to fight to get out of psychiatric hospital after her arrest. Ironically, it took her own faked suicide, and testimony from a doctor at the general hospital that she was *sane*, to get her out.

The terrible gap between women who are suffering some kind of mental torment and those elected to treat them is documented in books like Sylvia Plath's *The Bell Jar*. Sylvia describes her first visit to see 'Doctor Gordon', when she was feeling bleak and badly depressed. As she sits facing him, she is struck by a large family photo gleaming back at her from the desk: 'Then I thought, how could this Doctor Gordon help me anyway, with a beautiful wife and beautiful children and a beautiful dog haloing him like the angels on a Christmas card?'[13] Several women I spoke to who were interviewed by prison doctors, confided similar feelings of unease and even distrust. There was the constant suspicion that these people were not primarily concerned with helping them in the best way possible – but with administering treatment, which too often felt like further punishment.

Of the women who ended up in psychiatric hospital, several had been given ECT, a controversial shock treatment which is far less common than it was in the 1950s and 1960s. It is apparently an alarming experience, which some women remember only as a 'blankness', a wiping out of time. It boasts some successes, but an idea of the trauma behind it is given in *The Bell Jar*:

'Don't worry,' the nurse grinned down at me. 'The first time everybody's scared to death.'

I tried to smile, but my skin had gone stiff, like parchment.

Doctor Gordon was fitting two metal plates on either side of my head.

He buckled them into place with a strap that dented my forehead, and gave me a wire to bite.

I shut my eyes.

There was a brief silence, like an indrawn breath.

Then something bent down and took hold of me and shook me like the end of the world. Whee-ee-ee-ee, it shrilled, through an air crackling with blue light, and with each flash a great jolt drubbed me till I thought my bones would break and the sap fly out of me like a split plant.

I wondered what terrible thing it was that I had done.[14]

Janet Frame echoes the horror of ECT in *Faces in the Water*. Here, she has just finished a treatment: 'At first I cannot find my way, I cannot find myself where I left myself, someone has removed all trace of me. I am crying.'[15]

Treatment has become more sophisticated since those accounts were written. But the echo of fear does not fade so easily. Some of the women I interviewed personally had been admitted to hospital by consent of a relative, or by court order and were still very disturbed at the way they had been handled. Annette tells a cautionary tale. When she left her husband – after he had moved his pregnant lover in with them – she suffered a breakdown, which first manifested itself in her wandering aimlessly around the streets in her nightdress. The police contacted her husband, and he had her sent to a private nursing home. 'In this country', she says wryly, 'there are still places where you can pay to have your relatives put away.' The following six months, of repeated ECT and largactil in large doses, are lost months, vacuumed from her mind.

Annette committed minor arson later, and finally ended up in Broadmoor, a 'special hospital'. She was there for three years, during which time she slowly (and unaided by any form of psychotherapy) came to learn about her own responses, and the reasons for what had happened. The line between punishment and treatment is particularly fudged in Broadmoor, which sees itself as a 'hospital' and describes the officers as 'nurses' even though they are members of the Prison Officers' Association.

While in Broadmoor, Annette managed to visit women who have been locked away for years, including the 'most dangerous woman in Britain' – no-one can even remember what she is supposed to have done – who, after seventeen years of incarceration, had 'grey skin; not just pale, but grey. All her hair has fallen out. She is skin and bone.' Until Annette started to visit her, she was never let out. At her insistence, the officers relented, 'but she wasn't allowed to wear any clothes, and it had to be in the rain – because then, well, they wouldn't need to bother washing her.'

There are stories of brutalisation and rape in Broadmoor, ones which Annette says she can corroborate, but even the everyday level of sexual harassment can be intolerable. Candy was admitted to Broadmoor for repeated fire-setting. She was just nineteen, and terrified of the ill people she saw around her. One dinnertime she asked to be allowed to go off into a room on her own, 'to cry and think'. She was refused, and promptly put her fist through a window. Immediately she was removed, made to wear just a canvas gown – 'which was stained, due to my monthly' – and marched down some stairs. Here 'a male screw/nurse took the gown off and just put me in a cold, bleak room. I remember quickly trying to put on the clean gown and towel to hid my embarrassment. For six weeks, each morning you had to strip to wash – each time with two male staff watching. And again at night, each patient had to be stripped naked before they entered the room, always with male staff there. It was the most degrading thing I have ever experienced – they made a point of watching you too. It made you feel worthless and dirty. I vowed then that whatever it took I would leave this place one day and never return... To me, animals were treated with more respect than we were.' Candy was there for five years.

WOMEN BREAKING OUT

...There is a charge

For the eyeing of my scars, there is a charge
For the hearing of my heart –
It really goes.

And there is a charge, a very large charge
For a word or a touch
Or a bit of blood

Or a piece of my hair or my clothes
So, so, Herr Doctor
So, Herr Enemy.

Herr God, Herr Lucifer
Beware
Beware.

Out of the ash
I rise with my red hair
And I eat men like air.

> (Sylvia Plath, 'Lady Lazarus' in *Ariel*, Faber, 1968)

Anger and vengeance

Even in a chapter about 'madness' it is important to remember the essential rationality of most women who get involved in crime. Madness is a tag, a smear, a dismissal of the women underneath. Pat Arrowsmith remembers: 'I was in the old Holloway (before it was redesigned along psychiatric lines) and I got fed up with people saying women prisoners are all a little bit insane – "a bit touched up here". The new Holloway is built as a kind of hospital. But there are some women who are just fucking good crooks.'

Given that women are so easily labelled 'mad', it is perfectly feasible that some women can *use* this categorisation as a channel for protest and revenge. This is, of course, a dangerous game, and one which often backfires. But it is even more dangerous to ignore the anger and passion of 'mad' women. There is an eloquence here from which we all must learn. Some of the most powerful people in history – the witches – were condemned as mad women but, as Robin Morgan says in *Sisterhood is Powerful* (N.Y. Random House, 1970): 'You are a witch by being female, untamed, angry, joyous and immoral.' Witch was a label used to defeat women. But it was also a means of liberation from male values and judgements. Modern day witches are not bridled, or drowned, or chained to stocks, but they may well end up in psychiatric institutions.

'Madness' can be employed as a strategy for escape. Phyllis Chesler cites the case of Liebe Yentl, in Singer's *The Dead Fiddler*. 'Liebe Yentl', she explains, 'is able to avoid an unwanted husband through her "madness" – it is the only way she can. Only in "madness" can she also tyrannise her parents, inspire fear and respect, "name" reality as she sees it, criticize the community's hypocrisy, and engage in some very "unfeminine" behaviour: drinking, boasting, and dirty joke telling.'[16]

And although Nancy Spungen's desire for fame – or notoriety – was a deadly one, and ended in her own murder, she nonetheless was driven by a pulsing desire for a kind of freedom, a different reality to the suburban numbness she saw all around her. Says her mother, 'it was only natural that Nancy would like the Sex Pistols, want to be involved with them. They were angry and violent.' Says Nancy herself, 'I'm gonna die before I'm 21. I'm gonna go out in a blaze of glory. Like... like, *headlines*.'[17]

Like Nancy, Agnes, in *The Madness of a Seduced Woman*, suffered from too much ambition. 'I wanted the fire,' she proclaims, as she tells the story of how she shot another woman – the rival for her love – and was irresistibly drawn to the 'random principle of chaos loose in the world'.[18]

When women's 'madness' leads to crime, and crime to violence, society finds it impossible to comprehend. Because, says Emma, convicted of murdering her husband, 'When you're talking about women and crimes of violence, either they're seen as incredibly *sick*, because women aren't "naturally" violent (whereas a man just loses his temper and might lash out), or she's very cold and calculating' – the 'monster' of Lombroso's imaginings. When she first emerged from prison, and people asked her why she had done it, they expected penitence, guilt, confusion. One response they did not want to hear was that he deserved it. That a woman might take the law into her own hands and take control over her own destiny to such a dangerous and profound degree is a frightening prospect. Anger, after all, is a demon women are meant to avert in others, not cultivate in themselves.

Maria has a history of violent outbursts. Her childhood was troubled, her adolescence filled with confusion over her lesbian identity, and further complicated by involvement in the drug culture of the time: amphetamines and LSD. She has a constant feeling of physical threat against her – and yet is herself strong and prone to aggression. When she gets angry she hits out, which gives her an immediate feeling of release usually followed by the more acceptable female response of regret and remorse. When she describes her attacks, the roots seem to lie deep in disappointment at what life has dealt her. She is furious: and society must share the blame.

When she was a teenager, she went for a woman whom she thought was about to attack *her*: 'It was a nasty little stab, it were. But I felt elated. I felt great. I felt really good.' On another occasion, 'I attacked this girl, and just charged her like a rugby tackle, and I had her splattered all over the pavement. It wasn't even her that I was angry at. It was something that had happened and I just took it out on her'.

Finally, she lashed out at her own family after a trip abroad, and while suffering from frequent hallucinations due to drugs and lack of sleep. While staying at home Maria was woken with a start and, frightened to death by the unexpected movements of a relative in her room, and mistook it for an attack. She went berserk: 'I blamed my dad. I blamed all the family. I hit my father. I went for my brother with a knife... The next thing I knew I'd got the telephone wire round my mother's neck and pulled it as hard as I bloody could. I was throttling her.' Maria has been repeatedly hospitalised since – usually when she is clearly out of control and needs bringing down. She is labelled 'schizophrenic'; she is angry.

It is rare for women to be so openly expressive of violence. Their conditioned passivity persuades them against such 'masculine' behaviour. But there are other, equally 'big' ways of breaking out. Arson is one of the most spectacular. Forensic psychiatrist Dr John Taylor has made a study of women fire-setters, and says there are three main categories: schizophrenics – one woman he knew was being persecuted by the Pope, and had to 'smoke him out'!; teenage delinquents, who make fire to gain attention; and women who commit arson in the home, usually for revenge. Candy is certainly one of the second group, describing to me how she would set fire to cupboards and rubbish bins, and later to the art room of Holloway's occupational therapy department, in an urge to make someone notice her and take her seriously.

But June and Jennifer Gibbons, two black twins who have never spoken since childhood, except with each other, found a far grander release in their teenage fire-setting. Marjorie Wallace, in her book *The Silent Twins*, explains that 'This was the kind of catharsis they had been waiting for – a purification and redemption from their suffering. The flames shrieked out for all those years of frustration...'[19] They had ideas of being famous writers, but as young black women from a fairly humble background, realised that their chances of breaking through were limited. But always they dreamed – and when the dreams were of fire, they recognised them as 'symbols of escape from intolerable situations'. They have ended up in Broadmoor.

The 'intolerable situation' is often very simple: being female. Normal feelings of rebellion, ambition, desire, and nerve are soon dulled in many of girls, as they are socialised into being responsible, maternal, passive adult women. Psychiatrists, as much as everybody else, expect certain rigid patterns of behaviour from male and female. They even test patients for their 'masculinity' and 'femininity' quotients. But as Phyllis Chesler describes in *Women and Madness* – not every woman plays it meek and mild. 'Laverne: They gave me a lot of psychological tests and, you know, I came out "masculine". What does that mean? Like on one test they ask: "Do you want to be married and happy, or rich and single?" Oh shit – "rich and single" I said.' Wrong, wrong, wrong...

Subverting the system

Society cannot cope with women like Laverne, women, who, to quote social worker Patricia C, are 'larger than life'. Depending on class, education, determination and luck, these 'big' women could end up as feminist fighters and survivors, or criminals – or at worst psychiatric cases. Perhaps the only thing which differentiates the last from the first is, says Patricia C., that 'They feel the pain, but they don't have a philosophy for it.'

But many women develop strong survival strategies to fight a system which has them marked out as 'victim'. Even though she could easily have cracked up in prison, June 'just knew how to behave to survive. I knew what cover to take. Aggression has a lot to do with it. I'd take a lot, but you could feel the rage all the time, I'd make sure of that. And there *was* rage and anger there, that could at any time spill over onto somebody else.'

Even when their behaviour is condemned by psychiatrists or prison officers, women who really want to preserve their identity and individuality do so with a fantastic spirit of resistance. Mary, drug addict, prostitute, and lesbian, remembers years of damaging labels: 'I was always seen as disturbed and psychopathic and all that shit. One doctor said that whatever anyone did for me I kind of kicked them in the teeth. And I said, "Well, what's anyone ever done for me?" Psychiatrists are like that, aren't they? There's got to be a reason and a label, and everything comes down to sex. "When you find a man you'll stop using drugs and settle down and get married, and have kids" and all that shit. And I used to say "I'm alright. That's not a problem to me." Which I suppose convinced them I was disturbed, yeah!'

Anne was outraged when one psychiatrist told her she 'deserved' a long sentence for the accidental killing of her boyfriend. She fiercely defended her own sanity, and mocked any attempt to suggest otherwise. In Holloway she was examined by one of the doctors. 'He threw an inkblot on a piece of paper and he said: "What does that look like to you?" I said, "It looks like a fucking inkblot." Then he said, "Look into my eyes," and he had me heavy by both shoulders. And he said, "What can you see?" I said, "Your fucking glasses."

'The game he was playing with me – he was trying to put words in my mouth, to make me commit myself a "psycho", or whatever label he wanted on me.' And indeed, she was diagnosed a psychopath – an often used and arbitrary title conferred on many 'difficult' women. She was given a suspended three-year sentence, with a year in a therapy centre. Here again 'there was some silly twit of a psychiatrist telling me it was to do with my parents, and I just wouldn't listen.' In the end they let her go early – unable to stand the pressure!

Candy was also smart enough to recognise the doctor's intentions. Rather then reject his questions, she played along: 'I was out to shock and impress the doc. I told him no end of tales – how fire excited me. How I wanted to die...' Sexual theories about fire-setting are very popular among doctors, and the general public. Arsonists like Candy and Annette are not unaware of them – and are contemptuous. Annette: 'People are very scared of arson. And there are all these theories about it being sexual deviance... One friend even asked me if I got turned on by the firemen's uniforms! I didn't even think about anything like that. I honestly don't know why I did it.' When she first went into Broadmoor she really believed she would get some help. In the end it was *self*-help which pulled her through, a determination to face her own guilt and doubt and to get out in one piece. There are mental health groups which can offer women like this support, or discussion, run by radical practitioners and by women who have themselves been through psychiatric treatment, which were set up in the early 1980s in Britain and are London-based.[20] There are also therapy groups which can perhaps help to prevent crisis by looking at stress, and helping people to make positive changes in their lives, before the system swallows them up. The Women's Therapy Centre in London is one such organisation, whose work is described in *In Our Own Hands* by Sheila Ernst and Lucy Goodison (Women's Press, 1981). The two authors talk about the reasons for women's frequent depressions and mental illnesses: 'We have rarely been encouraged to decide what we want and to go for it openly, to be angry, powerful, demanding; nor to value our own needs as equal to other people's, especially those of men and children.' The aim of this alternative wave of 'therapy' is as much to challenge established terms and values as to offer direct help: 'It is a pity that we called it therapy. Therapy suggests a process aimed at adjusting women to conventional and restrictive roles; it suggests drug treatment to frighten and silence us. What we did was very different.'

Of course these feminist-inspired actions have led to a backlash among some of the traditional practitioners in psychiatry. D. E. Smith, quoted in *Women and the Psychiatric Paradox* (Open University Press, 1984) warns that women's protests against the status quo can often be classified as pathological *symptoms* – further proof, ironically, of female instability – so that potentially subversive statements are seen, conveniently, as 'merely "expressive", merely a movement – or a gesture, a raving, a hysteria, an attack on the dark *in* the dark, a bellow of rage or anguish, a horror of "not being" – that hole in the world through which its sense finally leaks away.' So feminism *itself*, with its insistence on women's autonomy and equality, is seen by some psychoanalysts – like Lundberg and Farnham, cited in the same book – as proof of illness and maladjustment!

But it is not all a story of abuse or neglect in the psychiatric profession by any means. The spirit of change is rising, in response to radical movements of the 1970s and 1980s. Some workers are trying to subvert the status quo within the system, and are working with their clients to create a more humane alternative. For women practitioners of psychiatry and psychology, the feminist movement has had a very positive effect on the way they can operate, and on the treatment of female clients. In America and Canada, workers in the mental health field have evolved new patterns of working. In 1975 a Task Force on women was set up within the Canadian Psychiatric Association, and started working at local and national levels to initiate changes in teaching, and to liaise with women in the community and profession. By 1980 the Canadian Psychological Association accepted firm guidelines on anti-sexist treatment of female clients, listed in detail in *Women and the Psychiatric Paradox*. These new criteria insisted that 'The therapist counsellor is willing to help the woman client to explore alternative options in addition to the culturally defined gender role. Besides marriage and motherhood, s/he acknowledges the importance of other activities in creating and solving women's problems.' Given the traditional feminine roles insisted upon by prison and psychiatric institutions generally, breakthroughs like these are tremendously important to women undergoing treatment.

Often common sense attitudes can avert a major crisis in a woman's life. Social worker Valerie cites one woman in Britain who has repeatedly asked to be sectioned: 'She stays in London, then she goes out and smashes windows; because she knows "I smash windows equals everybody comes round, and I get taken to hospital, and I get an awful lot of attention" – which is essentially what this woman needs, because there's not many people give her any validity, as a person.'

Valerie decided to stop the merry-go-round and simply ask her why she was behaving like this. 'I really felt this woman was having a spiritual crisis, and she comes to talk to me regularly now. For me what has been knocked fundamentally has been this woman's self-esteem: her capacity to believe that her own opinions are valid – but more than that, her capacity to believe that she can take charge of her own life.' She is, says Valerie, an intelligent, perceptive woman who just needs reminding that 'You mustn't underestimate your own internal resources.'

This straightforward philosophy is one she shares with other women workers in her team. As she explains, 'We're actually trying to give back to patients a sense of their own power.' It is precisely that potent human spirit which psychiatry too often numbs rather than cultivates. Valerie N. cites the case of a black woman who has been in psychiatric hospital for twenty years after reacting to an extremely disturbed family background. Gradually she is coming out of her shell – primarily because somebody has invested in her a sense of potential, after decades of wasted youth.

It would be naïve to suppose that such a simple method can counteract the profound distress of every 'mad' woman. Social worker Patricia C reminds us of the contradictions of psychiatric work, when she discusses a client of hers who stabbed her father ninety times after being persistently abused herself. For the present she cannot remember committing the act – but part of the social worker's job is to help bring her to that realisation. Is it worth it? Will the horror of the truth ever be transcended, however much faith is put in her resilience? Would it not be better in this case to leave her alone, with her self-protective delusions?

Each woman is different. Each psyche has its own levels of resistance – and its own scars to heal. But the time of dismissing someone as 'mad' is over. Better in most cases to try and mend the fracture, however delicate or risky the operation. Janet Gotkin spent years in and out of hospital, being tormented by the label of schizophrenia. In time, and with help, she came to reject the fatalistic prognosis of her doctors, and began to accept her divided self – and attempt to make it whole: 'I have learned from my own suffering that we must come to accept our many-faceted selves. That to alternate between extremes of ecstasy and lows of despair, to indulge in fantasy and vision, to act self-destructive or lethargic, to refuse to conform, to lunge forward in spasms of creativity only to retreat to depths of inactivity, to cry, to mourn, to suffer, to create new visions – is to be human, not sick.'[21]

Only a very small number of women who commit crime are actually labelled 'mad'. When they are, the mud sticks – and is spread over other criminal women, and the rest of the female sex. Some women *are* a physical danger to themselves and the public. Of course they must be contained. But many women are *not*. Remove the label, forget the stigma, and try to understand. Then the dangerous and the fearsome becomes that bit more 'normal' and comprehensible.' Madness as a category is a means of control over individuals. It is no longer helpful, or humane.

CHAPTER 5

Trial by media: popular images of women and crime

Behind the closed doors of prisons and psychiatric hospitals, women who commit crime certainly have damaging labels to bear: of 'badness', 'madness', and failed womanhood. But in public, under the critical eye of journalists, writers, programme-makers and artists, surely these carefully nurtured traditional notions are challenged and repudiated? Far from it. The media are as ignorant of criminal women as the authorities are condemnatory, and the main response to the whole question of female 'deviance' is – silence. Until recently there has been very little serious discussion on television or in the newspaper about women's role in crime, although men who break the law are constant headline runners, and favourite fodder for newsworthy crime scares. When women *are* the focus of media attention they do not shed the harmful labels so beloved by police and courts – but they actually gain a few for good measure.

Mainstream media images of the criminal woman serve to mirror, highlight and reinforce the female stereotypes set up by conventional society, with stories of 'innocent' young women, of 'sexy mistresses', of 'protective mothers', and, if all else fails, of terrifying, unfathomable 'monsters'. These lurid characterisations confirm what men want to hear about women, and process them into neat little boxes – defusing any potential threat by creating recognisable, flawed, fallible females. Things are slowly changing, with an increased political awareness of women's independent role in all walks of life – including crime – permeating the alternative media, and slowly affecting the 'straight' image-makers too. But the 'new' picture of the female criminal is a complex one, still undermined in many instances by the old 'frailty-thy-name-is-woman' preconceptions.

How different it is for the men. Where newspaper editors will struggle to find a chink in the female criminal's armour, they are equally as keen to bolster the idea of iron-hard machismo in talking about men who break the law. The male criminal is to be feared, loathed, loved, or at least respected. He is, in his media persona, the epitome of what a traditional he-man ought to be. As Colin MacInnes wrote in a critical essay twenty years ago, 'The intense interest in crime among all sections of society is suspect. The don deep in his (sic) murder book, the millions rapt in sex stories of their Sabbath papers, the key place (male) criminals hold in literature, film and television, whether vulgarised or intellectual, all attest that in some sense, the criminal is the hero of our times.'[1]

DO WE NEED ANOTHER HERO?

There are big bucks to be made by writing about men and crime. Norman Mailer's book about U.S. murderer Gary Gilmore, *The Executioner's Song*, is a blockbuster seller, and, as the back cover blurb proudly proclaims, has made Gilmore himself 'a media star'. London gangland leaders Reggie and Ronnie Kray regularly crop up in television and theatre satire – and there have been television series galore about cops and criminals: from the sharp-shooting *Miami Vice* and the avuncular *Rockford Files* to the lovable British prison series *Porridge*, and Cockney spoof *Minder*.

Although many of these money-spinners rely on humour in their male characters, there is, just as often, an emphasis on danger and risk. Media criminals embody the rebellious man – supposedly every boy's adolescent dream, and every girl's sexual fantasy. Film writer Jane Root describes 'the graphic and extreme sadism which is a vital component of most recent prison films' – films like *Scum* and *Midnight Express* – something explained to her by the producers as a 'deterrent' but more likely to be a voyeuristic catharsis, or even an endorsement of such behaviour to its audience.[2]

There is also a whole genre of books which revels in the murderous exploits of some real-life male criminals. The authors pretend to be factual, but they actually elaborate in a rather sickening way on these facts, to create an unpleasant fictional element, and an unpalatable male mythology. Emlyn Williams' *Beyond Belief* (Pan, 1968), written in 1968 about the Moor Murders case – in which Ian Brady and Myra Hindley were convicted of murdering three children – is a classic example. Much of the book is conducted in a patronising mock-Northern accent, and lulls the reader into false security and familiarity, before wallowing in semi-factual, semi-surmised details about the murders. Williams constantly emphasises Brady's satanic presence, and Hindley's submission to her murderous 'master', and he finally builds the reader up to feel a titillating, stomach-churning fear and paranoia. Gordon Burns' *Somebody's Husband, Somebody's Son* (Pan, 1985) which describes the life of mass murderer Peter Sutcliffe, the 'Yorkshire Ripper', so-called for his murderous assaults on thirteen women in the late 1970s, follows a similar pattern. He dwells on the dour Yorkshire atmosphere, and the lurking obsessions of the young Sutcliffe – his fear of venereal disease and furious belief in female sexual evil – to evoke disgust and loathing right from the start.

These sordid, impressionistic accounts of infamous criminals, like the television fictions, reinforce the idea of dangerous manhood, of 'heroes' and 'anti-heroes', whose anger is absolute, whose toughness is unassailable. The real picture is, of course, very different. Sociologist Laurie Taylor remembers his first meeting with ex-bankrobber John McVicar, when he was surprised that 'there was no sign, at least as yet, of the "thin, snarling lips" which the *Mirror* had thought so significant ...' And McVicar himself, says Taylor, 'knew there was something mythical about the usual picture of the big-time robber. He'd spent years trying to distance himself from the press description of his dangerousness.'[3] Distorted images like this do the criminalised *woman*, let alone the man, no good at all. They create a stark divide which implies that while male criminals are larger-than-life, and almost mythical in their menace, women are simply manipulated helpmates, or victims, or, once more, just invisible ciphers. In the face of such virile 'Rambo' types, when women *do* come under the spotlight, they appear that much less threatening or powerful. Instead, their 'deviance' is, in contrast, carefully controlled by media-makers, to make it fit into all the conventional, prissy, petulant, 'feminine' moulds. So female deviance actually becomes feminine submission. Or so it is hoped.

THE FANTASY FEMALE: MISTRESS; MOTHER; MONSTER

Present-day newspaper stories

'Women get a very shabby deal from the media. It's a real case of knitting as the guillotine falls. A client whom I'd known for some time – she'd been here, and had committed a not very pleasant crime, but nonetheless... On her release the *Daily Mirror* used a distorted shot of her, "the evil Mary Smith" (pseudonym). I couldn't recognise her as the person I'd worked with for five months.' (Richard Ford, women's bail hostel, London)

As with the men, newspapers are reluctant to cover the subject of women who are actively involved in crime in any serious, straightforward fashion: the statistics are so low, and the crimes themselves relatively 'petty'. Shoplifting and fraud are just not – to use Fleet Street jargon – 'sexy', saleable stories. But when they *do* latch onto something, then the emphasis is either on shock-horror (as with Richard Ford's client – the 'unnatural, monstrous hag' tag) or on standard pictures of women taken to an imaginative extreme – evoking 'mistressly' excesses of promiscuity, and 'motherly' displays of emotional dependence. Very different to the movie hero image. If the stories are not about sexual manipulation or female devotion, then they emphasise sweet innocence, or wild hysteria – violently contradictory images, all of them, and applied to women by the popular media, criminal or not.

A classic crime story for reporters must evoke the absolute 'he man' who mugs, rapes, kills – or the archetypal she-woman. She is young, naïve, harmless – like Kay Doddington, who, so the *Sun* of July 29, 1985, tells us, in a story headlined, WOOLLIES FIRE KAY OVER 2P FUDGE, 'was sacked and reported to the police – for stealing a sweet worth TWO PENCE'; or she is the 'drama queen' stereotype, reported on a few days later in the *London Standard*. 'Sheila'. blabbed an excited caption writer, under a faded family photograph and news story, 'is the beautiful daughter who has brought so much joy to her family as she stands on the threshold of a glamorous career as a model... Eight years later, on August 7, 1985, the family was destroyed when, in a frenzy, Sheila killed her twin six-year-old sons, then turned a rifle on her mother and then her father ... and finally on herself.' Sheila is marked here as a tragic desperate heroine, trapped in her own excess of emotion, and posthumously a star for the *Standard*. (Ironically, the case was later re-opened and Sheila's culpability proved false.)

Mention the word 'actress' to a crime reporter and his pen immediately lights up. First, it means sex and showbiz (licence to go over the top). Second, the term is frequently used in court about women, particularly in sexual harassment cases, to undermine their evidence, and suggest their ability to manipulate, and to lie.

Helen Rose, an actress who took 'tycoon' Liam Keane to court on charges of attempted rape in July 1985 really got a newsprint battering. When the case was still in progress, the *Sun* had already made its own verdict with the headline, judiciously put in quotes, ACTRESS 'DREAMED UP FANTASY LOVER'. The inference that she had made the whole thing up – as Keane successfully claimed in court – is nudged further along in the *Sun* by picking out 'sexy' irrelevant facts: 'Helen... said she had appeared in twelve films, including the sex comedy *Percy's Progress...*'

The jury acquitted Keane the day after this. And then even the sober 'quality' newspaper, the *Daily Telegraph* (August 2, 1985), got excited – ACTRESS'S RAPE CRY 'WAS HER BEST ROLE' – and told how the Old Bailey jury heard that this case was 'the best role she had had for a long time'.

Whether victim or not to Keane's sexual advances, Helen Rose never got the benefit of the doubt: that one word 'actress', immediately signalled her sexual duplicity and unreliability – for the newspapers, and for the jury.

Jacki Holborough, interviewed in chapter 1 about her innocent involvement in an international conspiracy, suffered similar treatment from the press in 1977. Although there were *four other people* in the dock with her (all much more implicated in the case than she) the *London Evening News* chose to pick out Jacki. Why? Because of her profession... Front-page banner headline on April 18, 1977: FLASH FRED AND ACTRESS IN £1M PLOT. Eager to bring showbiz into what was actually a complicated, technical story, the *Evening News* proceeded: '"Flash Fred fascinated me", says actress Jacki.' 'Miss Holborough... who formerly appeared in the Crossroads tv series is one of five people in the dock...'

So taken in by all this were the courtroom spectators, that one of Jackie's friends heard someone in the gallery whisper, 'She's giving the performance of her life.' 'Slim', 'blonde', and 'on the stage' – Jacki never stood a chance from the word go. The jury sent her down.

Sex and politics sell newspapers. Mix the two together and you have dynamite: so the tabloids in August 1985 made whoopee with a kiss-and-tell story by 'kissogram beauty' who talked about 'my topless night with MPs'. And some women themselves make capital out of editors' salacious tastes. Thus Christine Keeler, involved in a fateful triangle between Jack Profumo, British minister for war in 1961, and Eugene Ivanov, a Russian diplomat, although contemptuous, all these years later, of the major press and government scandal at the time, in which 'leading participators... were helpless victims', nonetheless went to print in 1985 with her own book *Sex Scandals* – half to defuse myths around the Profumo Affair, but half to revel in *other* women's 'scandals'. (Choice tales in the book include: 'The Black Book and the Cult of the Clitoris', and 'The Sexy Vicar – or The Road to Blackpool'.) This kind of thing makes it much harder to loosen the grip of fantasy from fact, and reach the real women. They themselves have been seduced by the media images which distort them.

The press are happiest, and at their most sanctimonious, when they can suggest a saintly, madonna image of women, either with child at the breast, or in faithful support of a husband. Even when the story is one of fighting back, as with Freda Paterson, who, after a lifetime suffering his brutality, stabbed her husband to death, the media can still pull an acceptable passive image from the bag. So the *Sun* (October 1984), under the shock banner headline SLAVE WIFE TURNED KILLER, describes the husband as 'Burly Peter Paterson, a hard drinking brewers' drayman', while she is still simply his 'tiny, greyhaired wife'.

The more diminutive and fragile the female, the better, especially if she acts as innocent foil to a tough male criminal. So the *Sunday Mirror* (August 4, 1985) was particularly delighted with the little girl who visited gangster Reggie Kray in his top security jail, where he was busy raising money for her liver transplant. 'TRAGIC LIVER GIRL VISITS KILLER KRAY', they cried, and she even calls him 'Uncle Reg'! Even killers soften their hearts when a little girl works her magic...

Asian women are often pushed into a particularly humiliating image of servile motherliness in the British media – whether they are the ever-willing hostesses who smile sweetly from Air India ads, or the vulnerable sari-clad deportees, snapped at Heathrow Airport, surrounded by children, frightened and isolated, before being forcibly sent 'back home'.

The image of these women took a new turn, however, in the Afia Begum case in August 1983. Afia was refused entry to Britain when her husband died, just before she arrived to join him here. When she lost her appeal to stay, and was thus forced into a quasi-criminal role by remaining, she went into hiding with her two-year-old daughter. But this could not be turned into just another 'poor refugee on the run' story. Asian women activists, the 'Sari Squad', chained themselves to Home Secretary Leon Brittan's house, at the start of a well-run campaign to get the appeal decision reversed. And as the Women, Immigration and Nationality Group (WING) explained: 'The Sari Squad campaigned in a way which stressed the militancy and strength of black women, rather than portraying us as possible victims incapable of fighting for ourselves.'

Immigration officers finally raided Afia's hiding place and returned her to Bangladesh – though the Sari Squad went on to campaign throughout Europe. Writer Prathibha Parmar[4] contrasts this case with that of the Pereira family. Living in a Hampstead village, at the time of the Begum case, this Asian family had overstayed their residence permits.

When threatened with deportation, they were supported by the white villagers (including the clergy) where they lived, and were finally granted permission to stay. Unlike Afia, portrayed as 'alien' and unfamiliar, these people were seen as assimilated, manageable – almost white. The *Daily Express* (May 23, 1984) described them as 'perfect immigrants', and a Rear Admiral friend considered the father 'a thoroughly reliable chap'. Afia, a woman alone, with her back-up of Asian militancy, did not fit into the prescribed polite newspaper image – but subverted it in a potentially powerful way.

But even though some women appear to defy conventional categories, the media pulls them into line, just the same. Even when women are involved in serious politically motivated crime, there are ways of controlling the images to make them seem less frightening, less monstrous – even to become 'sexy'. The British media foam at the mouth at the mere mention of the Irish Republican Army. So in November 1984, when the *Standard* revealed the name of Evelyn Glenholmes, a woman implicated in a bomb attack on Chelsea Barracks, London, back in 1981, they savoured the moment fully, with a front page 'artist's impression', showing the 'blonde bomber' as thick, stocky and brutal, and dubbing her 'Britain's most wanted woman'. But her implied 'butchness' didn't stop them quoting the Head of the Anti-Terrorist Branch in the same article, declaring her to have 'a very good figure...'

Back in 1977 the *Daily Mail* put paid to gang robber Christine Morris. No mean criminal, she had been involved in 597 offences, carrying off £75,000 from her latest adventure. At the hands of skilful subeditors, Ms Morris became a sexy sop to her accomplices. 'Redhead Christine Morris is a fast worker... But Morris, wearing a low-cut green jumper and no bra, confessed it wasn't *all* her own work.' By the end of the piece, her rebellion was transformed into pathos. 'There were tears in Morris's eyes as Detective Constable Richard Gardiner described her past... how she ran away from home at fifteen and went to live with "undesirables" in Birmingham.' From bigtime robber, Christine Morris was reduced to sex symbol – and finally to little, lost, adolescent girl.

Although in a very different area of crime, and at the other end of the age scale, Rosie Jones also fell prey, in 1984, to the media's patronising methods. After 20 years in prison, on and off, doing a nifty line in pickpocketing, Rosie, 75, decided to call it a day, after getting a conditional discharge for her latest crime. 'Freedom is better than diamonds says granny', ran the *Standard*'s headline in 1984. The article gleefully listed the various ailments which persuaded Rosie to give up thieving, underlining her fragility, and noting with satisfaction that she 'wiped away a few tears' at her release, before hobbling home. She may have been a naughty girl in her time – but now she was just a frail old dear.

Where white and Asian women are often brought under control by emphasising their basic passivity, Afro-Caribbean women are just as victimised by an opposite image of them as 'mouthy' and 'aggressive'. So when 800 women hit a small seaside resort on an organised shoplifting swoop – a crime normally associated with lonely, depressed, menopausal white women – the *Sun* (July 31, 1985) could not resist the rider that the 'eighteen coachloads of women' (who carried off thousands of pounds worth of stuff) were 'mainly black'. Whether true or not (and the *Sun* was the only paper to break this extraordinary story) the implication was subtly menacing: black hordes swoop on peaceful seaside town.

Sometimes the press are less pleased to parade their headlines. Jenny Hicks, convicted in 1976 on post office fraud charges (see chapter 1), does not remember a particular press splash over her case. Why? She feels it was 'probably too close to the bone', since company fraud happens all the time, among the most 'respectable' of the business world. Her profession, as successful business woman, lent itself less easily to sexy innuendo, although she does remember one blatant headline – REDHEAD LICKS THE POST OFFICE, which conveniently ignored her partner in fraud – who happened to be a man, haircolour unknown. In the courtroom itself it was Jenny who was billed by the prosecuting counsel as an 'evil presence' – the malevolent one – while *he* was described simply and in dashing terms as the 'young company director'.

For most of this case it was a judicious silence from the press. Lesley Whittle, a fragile-looking young heiress who had been kidnapped at the same time as Jenny Hicks' court case, made more juicy copy, and hit many more headlines. The press can *always* cope better with woman as passive victim, than as an active agent in crime.

Images from history

'Woman throughout the ages has been mistress to the law, as man has been its master.' (Freda Adler)

There is some truth in the idea that women have been treated more leniently for their crimes than men. Their presupposed vulnerability and enforced dependence effectively disembarred them from being treated responsibly; from being 'master' of their own identity. But as Ann Jones comments in *Women Who Kill,* her blockbuster about nineteenth-century murderesses (and murder is the most chronicled female crime in popular archives – it being the most sensational), this favouritism under criminal law was a cunning pay-off for the almost total lack of rights in *civil* matters. However, looking at cases from previous centuries, the 'rewards' of being a woman and committing crime rarely seemed worth the patronising – and sometimes deadly – penalties.

Possibly the worst punishments ever inflicted on women en masse in the West took place during the witchcraze of the fifteenth, sixteenth and seventeenth centuries. Vast numbers of women were tortured, and killed, for the 'crime' of supposed anti-Christian activities and sexual impurities. They were made to confess to terrible, fantastical obscenities, like eating children's hearts, fucking with the 'devil', and murdering old people in ghastly rituals. These were all fabrications by their persecutors. The victims were usually single, and therefore a threat to the idea of marriage and male ownership. The net of persecution was spread so wide that, as Mary Daly writes, 'clearly, the intent was to break down and destroy strong women'. Often the women were not even accused of specific crimes for, as Mary Daly says, 'The point, of course, is not to punish crime, because there was no crime. The point is "to appease the wrath of God"'.[6] To purify unclean women. This notion of filth in the female body is a religious one – and has crossed over to the legal system through the centuries. The notion of 'innocence defiled' appears, in muted form, in modern day reporting as well as in medieval screeds.

There was a hypocritical twist to the law's paternalism in the 1700s. While leniency was granted for women involved in cases of capital treason, or for women who were pregnant, it certainly was *not* allowed in cases of murder in marriage. Excuses about feminine gullibility and vulnerability did not extend to husband and home. Here, a man was a true king, and his dethronement termed 'petty treason'. For this a woman would be burned *and* hanged – just to make sure she got the point.

As Michael Ignatieff pointed out in 'Hanging Women' (*Observer*, July 10, 1983), an article looking at punishment through the ages and showing how various women fell for, or escaped, the noose, lipservice in the law towards chivalry often seemed fainthearted and superficial. In 1786 Phoebe Harris was convicted of coining (faking money). She was, for her pains, one of the last women to go to the stake in England – hanged and then burned. If she had been a man, says Ignatieff, she would have met the even more gory fate of being quartered and disembowelled... Not pleasant ways to go, either way. Phoebe was dispatched more cleanly perhaps – but dispatched just the same.

The methods of death for murderers got a little less bloody in the following century, and the killing went on discreetly behind walls. Public hangings were abolished in 1868, with Charles Dickens a leading abolitionist. But the law, press and public were all – on the surface at least – rather squeamish, in Victorian times, about the hanging of errant women. The predominant notion of Victorian womanhood was one of middle-class gentility. Even the methods of murder by women – usually poison – had a delicate, vaporous tinge to them. Notions of mistressly innocence were clung to, whenever possible. In cases of male-female teamwork, says author Ann Jones, the man had to take the rap: '...When a man and woman seemed to be accomplices in murder, men found it reassuring to pin the crime on the man and to ignore the woman's motives and her ability to act.'

Even where a woman seemed undisputably guilty, the public – and media – of the time would often back her up and declare her innocence. Mary Hartmann, in a socially critical (but nonetheless pretty salacious) book about Victorian murderesses involved in 'unspeakable crimes'[7] tells the story of one middle-class teenage girl who, quite literally, seemed to get away with murder.

In 1859 seventeen-year-old Madeline Smith fell in love with one Emile L'Angelier, 26, and conducted a steamy passion with him – chronicled by 60 letters, *all* of which were read out in court, (a sort of nineteenth-century soap opera) revealing 'a relationship which captivated a Victorian public with an already keen appetite for crime and sexual adventure in high places'. Madeline's passion ultimately began to pall, especially in the face of a marriage proposal from someone else – of much higher station. Unable to shake L'Angelier off, the story goes, she resorted to poison, polishing him off with a dose of arsenic. When questioned about traces of the deadly dust on her own person, she declared, wide-eyed, that it was merely 'face powder'. The jury, in 'one of the most sensational trials of the century', acquitted Ms Smith, unable to accept that she had had sex both before marriage, and *willingly*, with this lowly, hapless specimen, Emile. Says Mary Hartmann, 'Newspapers, pamphlets, legal reviews, and even religious publications, either stoutly maintained her innocence or else defended her to taking righteous revenge against a depraved fortune hunter and seducer.'

When confronted by other women who took their destiny into their own hands, like Hannah Kinney, who in 1840 was accused of poisoning her husband (a heavy drinker and gambler), lawmakers got scared by the abandonment of faithful femininity. Images of 'sweet wives' disappeared, and dragons and demons were dredged up. Could a beautiful, high-ranking woman like Hannah Kinney really behave in this bestial way? As Ann Jones reports, Hannah's defence attorney cleverly manipulated the demonic image to Hannah's advantage, saying dramatically: 'If that woman is a murderer, she is a moral monster, such as the world never saw! There is no sentence your verdict can impose, and no punishment the law can give, that is adequate to such a crime. No, gentlemen; human nature could not compass it, and human intelligence cannot believe it.' Anxious to maintain the illusion of happily married middle-class womanhood, and for their own peace of mind, the all-male jury acquitted her.

But woe betide the likes of Maria Manning, a much less easily manipulated creature, as Michael Ignatieff reports, and too far from the discreet beauty of Hannah Kinney to be pardoned. Abandoning the polite mores of bourgeois women, Maria Manning not only took on an extramarital affair, but then bashed her lover over the head with a poker and ran off with his money. And all this was done in cahoots with her cuckolded husband! Not surprisingly, public sensibility at the time could not handle this 'immoral' defiance. She went to the gallows, together with her husband in 1849, screaming to the last: 'Shame! There is no law and justice to be gathered here! Base and degraded England!' Clearly this was a 'monster' too defiant to live, and the middle-class moralism of the law was too hypocritical to let her.

The prettier Victorian images of womanhood prevailed well into this century. You can sniff the smelling salts on newspaper crime reports from the 1900s up to as late as the 1950s. Edgar Lustgarten, an appropriately named popular crime writer, dug out a tearjerker from 1914 for his *Evening Standard* column (April 27, 1977). A certain Miss Jefferson was sueing Mr Paskell for breach of promise: he had refused to marry her when she contracted consumption. Discounting a fair amount of callousness on Paskell's part, Lustgarten waxes lyrical: 'Theirs is a tale only of wooing and of woe... The jury would be desperately sorry for Miss Jefferson. Desperately anxious to do *something* for her.' The 'something' was a well-earned £500 damages. She could have done without the attendant condescension. It's interesting that Lustgarten chooses this sort of story with which to fondly reminisce. Around the same era, suffragettes were setting fire to letterboxes, churches – even their own prison cells. It would be hard to get so coy about *that* image of women.

But the 'monsters' still lurked, to defy Lustgarten's pathetically passive images. As late as 1944 Mrs Helen Duncan was being prosecuted under the Witchcraft Act of 1735 – 'witch' being an age-old and popular way of branding wayward women. She certainly sounded pretty weird – claiming that she could produce ectoplasm from eyes, ears and noses, and turn them into spirits. She was sentenced to nine months on the rather more mundane charge of fraud. But note the difference in tone – from the fragile Miss Jefferson to Old Bailey Clerk Leslie Boyd's graceless description of Mrs Duncan as 'a gargantuan twenty stone medium' (*Evening News* reminiscences, April 21, 1977).

Leaping a decade to the 1950s and from a 'demon' to a picture of helpless innocence, an enigmatic reporter J.A.J., writing a crime column in the *Evening News* ('Courts Day By Day', April 21, 1955) provides a story spiced with every ounce of condescension traditionally employed towards women in times past and present, whether criminal or not. It is worth quoting at length to show how hard it is for media men to believe that women are rational *or* independent, fully grown-up *or* responsible. It is the most ludicrous piece of journalism I've ever read, and, in one form or another, it still goes on.

J.A.J. relates how, in 1955, Gladys, a 'girl' of 18, stole two shillings from the nursery where she worked. When brought before the courts (presumably terrified for her job, and completely out of her class and depth) she uttered no word in her defence, a fact J.A.J. finds appealing and perplexing:

> The baffling thing about men and women is that you can never tell what they are really like by looking at them. There are handsome men who are not blackguards. And some extremely ugly men do not possess hearts of gold. But the women make the men seem as transparent as glass. If you can guess correctly at first glance a woman's make up under her make-up then you are even cleverer

than those weighing machines at the seaside which by the aid of science and a penny produce infallible judgements at a moment's notice such as 'You have a kind nature, you are fond of dancing and knitting, and you should beware of dark men!'

Which brings us logically enough to the story of Gladys. Gladys is as slender as all girls of 18 ought to be, and she has hair the colour of ripening corn, and her eyes are as blue as bluebells and when the clerk of the East End court asked her if she was guilty she said 'Yes'. 'You stole two shillings?' 'I'm afraid I did sir.'

After this, certain facts were read out by the policeman who arrested Gladys:

'Well, sir', said the woman detective, who was as unreadable to the layman as any other woman, 'all the people in the nursery were asked to turn out their pockets, and the coin was found in the girl's purse and she admitted stealing it!'

The court, says J.A.J., tried desperately to unearth more details about her:

But Gladys could not, or would not, help to solve the mysteries that are hidden by bluebell eyes and corn coloured hair. 'I'm very sorry sir,' she blushed.

Put on probation by a benevolent magistrate – but having lost her dignity and her livelihood – Gladys is duly humbled and humiliated, by the court and by the press:

'Thank you, sir' whispered Gladys, and she went out into the streets of a London populated by eight million mysteries.

Famous scapegoats

Public imagination is always fired by lurid stories about prisoners fighting for their lives in Death Row, or incarcerated for ever on charges of particularly heinous crime. It is a world of notoriety that seems so far from our own, and it's fun to point the finger, or emit sighs of futile sympathy, from the comfort of a living room, safe and sound. Durkheim has pointed out that 'the deviant person is created by and necessary to the community, both as a focus for group feelings and as an indicator of prevailing social boundaries of attitudes and behaviour'. In other words – we all love and need a scapegoat.

'Infamous' females fill that need more dramatically than men, since they 'deviate' further from the accepted norm. Two women stand out in British memory as particularly notorious scapegoats: Ruth Ellis, hanged for murder in 1955, and Myra Hindley, jailed for life, for child murder, in 1966. These fallen icons reappear periodically in the news: long dead Ruth Ellis is star of a new film, and Myra Hindley, less glamour-worthy, has regular parole pleas regularly turned down. Their crimes, murder of a lover, and murder of children, excite, respectively, passionate interest and savage repulsion. News of these women allows us our ritual bloodletting, but effectively stops us thinking about what really lies behind those cardboard media images.

Ruth Ellis: the mistress

'Six revolver shots shattered the Easter Sunday calm of Hampstead and a beautiful platinum blonde stood with her back to the wall. In her hand was a revolver...' (*Daily Mail*, April 29, 1955)

This could be the opening paragraph of a raunchy thriller, but is actually a contemporary news report of a famous murder. On July 13, 1955, Ruth Ellis, the 'platinum blonde' above, was the last woman to be hanged in Britain. She was a nightclub hostess, convicted of shooting her upper-class lover David Blakely at point blank range. It was a case which the courts and the papers tried to make into a classic 'crime passionnel'. They failed miserably, because Ruth Ellis had the temerity to remain calm and unemotional in court, with no displays of confusion or remorse. She was already dubbed a 'bad' woman – by being a mistress in button-lipped England of the 1950s (though of course 'bad' women have their function too, in terms of public titillation). But because of her innate composure, both throughout the trial and at the moment of death (public hangman Albert Pierrepoint later said that 'she was the bravest woman I ever hanged') Ruth Ellis thwarted social expectations of just what a 'bad woman' should be. She struggled for her integrity, and was pilloried in the process by a vindictive press.

Tabloids of the 1980s are content to scream out a few punchy headlines and wallow in selected salacious details of crime cases. But the press in the 1950s was far more sober and long-winded about court reporting. Often long transcripts of trials were printed – and in the case of Ruth Ellis, these reports are most revealing.

One of the initial fascinations of this affair for an English society riddled by class consciousness, was, as film writer Chris Auty has remarked,[8] that people 'never understood why an upper middle-class man and a lower middle-class woman should fall so obsessively in love'. This was a story as much about snobbery as about passion.

When the case opened, the *Daily Mail* (April 22, 1955) leaned heavily on Blakely's superior pedigree – where he was educated, the fact that he was son of a doctor, and his glamorous ambition to become a 'top' racing driver. They even added details of his funeral – attended by many 'leading motorists'. This was high society. Ruth, in contrast, was described bluntly as a '28-year-old model'. Then, later, to rub her nose in it, come patronising embellishments: 'Her hair was short, stylish, her dress exclusive, but she failed to rid herself of a Manchester accent… She felt it a barrier to Mayfair.' She even took elocution lessons, we hear, 'But every turn failed, for Blakely was still ashamed of her.'

Having stripped her of any social dignity, *Daily Mail* reports then faithfully reproduced court evidence of her sexual promiscuity, constantly referring to her 'simultaneous love affairs' with a man called Desmond Cussen as well as David Blakely, in order to undermine her genuine feelings towards the latter. She came over in reports as the epitome of the 'jealous tart': Blakely had been trying to end his connection with her, and Ruth Ellis became angry, 'even though she had another lover at the time'.

So far the story filled conventional expectations, and the court was building up an image of a lower-class, love-crazy creature, risking all for an ill-fated romance with a young gentleman way 'above' her class. The next step was to prove her emotional instability as a woman. This is where the image fell apart.

The defence did its best to evoke sympathy for Ruth Ellis, helped by a soothing headline from the *Mail*: 'This woman found herself in an emotional prison', and psychiatrist Dr Duncan Whittaker issued a standard statement at her trial to explain her behaviour: 'A woman was more prone to hysterical reaction than a man in the case of infidelity, and in such circumstances could lose her critical faculties and try to solve the problem at a more primitive level.'

But he had to admit that when he interviewed her in her cell, she had behaved with complete 'equanimity' – and when defence counsel Melford Stevenson asked her of her intentions when she shot Blakely – possibly to provoke confessions of confusion and terror – she replied quite simply, quite unhysterically: 'It is obvious. When I shot him I intended to kill him.' Her sanity could not now be disputed, no leniency allowed. Her guilt was pronounced, and the death sentence passed. Polite and composed to the last, Ruth Ellis smiled her thanks. She wanted to die.

The British press was consummately shocked by this behaviour. 'Model *smiles* at murder verdict' ran the *Mail* headline next morning, its disapproval implicit in the following report:

> Mrs Ruth Ellis turned to a nurse attendant in the dock at the Old Bailey yesterday and smiled as the jury announced their verdict: guilty of murder. . . . That smile was the first sign of emotion the 28-year-old platinum blonde had given during her trial. . .

Despite the public outcry over the hanging of a woman, which offended modern sensibilities and prompted eminences like Arthur Koestler and Victor Gollancz to campaign for its abolition, there was bafflement and common displeasure at the 'cold' way Ruth Ellis had behaved. Witnesses of the trial harboured a grudge against her for years after, even though she had paid the price of her crime with her life. Robert Hancock in his book *Ruth Ellis: The Last Woman to be Hanged*,[9] says contemptuously of her that she described the shooting 'like a male motorist reporting the running down of a stray dog'. And in 1977 Leslie Boyd, Clerk of the Court at her trial, wrote disparagingly:

I studied her closely throughout the trial and thought she was a cold-blooded murderess. She was an extremely attractive woman with rather brittle-looking blonde hair...

It was hard to accept that she had deliberately pumped several bullets into her lover at pointblank range...

When the sentence was passed some people close to her said she whispered 'Thanks'. I can well believe that. I don't think Ruth Ellis really cared. (*Evening News*, April 18, 1977)

No-one could understand what really motivated this woman to kill. She did not live up to her 'crazy whore' image, so carefully constructed by law court and media, and so she was doubly condemned. But the legacy of Ruth Ellis has recently come under renewed scrutiny in Mike Newell's subtle film *Dance with a Stranger*, scripted by Shelagh Delaney (Britain, 1985). This artistic reconstruction of her life follows some of the clues left unexamined by contemporary reports and shows – without false sentimentality or uncritical support – some of the factors which could have made Ruth Ellis commit murder.

Dance with a Stranger depicts Ruth's life after meeting Blakely, and ends at his shooting. It shows the same 'brittle blonde' of the trial, but looks behind the mask to reveal a woman being slowly crucified by her addiction to a lover both contemptuous of, and dependent on her: he is privileged by status and money, where she is bereft of both. She kills because she can bear the contradictions and tensions no longer. She is 'brittle' because she must fight to gain control over her life, and later, to win dignity before a hostile court and press. Mike Newell's interpretation of her insists not on Ruth's surface coldness, so pilloried by the contemporary commentators, but on her underlying integrity.

A prisoner of the society which condemned her, Ruth was just as convinced as everyone else – even relieved – that she should die. In a letter written to Blakely's mother while in Holloway awaiting death, a letter not headlined in contemporary reports, but flashed up, tellingly, on the screen before the final credits of *Dance with a Stranger*, she wrote 'I shall die loving your son, and you should feel content that his death has been repaid.'

Ruth Ellis went to the gallows, not just because she shot a man. She died because she did not fit the sexy stereotype she seemed, with her working class, 'common' background and platinum hair, so perfectly suited for. She died because, as Chris Auty says, 'The law, so apparently impartial, takes vengeance when the lower classes refuse to humble themselves, or acknowledge their place.' She died because she did not plead for mercy, and because she was not sorry. She died because she made fools of those members of press and public who wanted a soiled, identikit anti-heroine to take pity on, and were confronted instead with a complex, intelligent human being.

Myra Hindley: the monster

Myra Hindley has been a one-woman British scapegoat for all things criminally 'evil' since 1966, when she was convicted with her lover, Ian Brady, of child murder, murder which he initiated and to which she was accomplice. Both were sentenced to life imprisonment and remain inside to this day.

While Ian Brady comes across as a dangerous psychopath (he has recently been transferred from prison to a special psychiatric unit), both in Emlyn Williams' book on the subject, and in the rare newspaper reports about him, Myra Hindley is portrayed as being more complicated, and infinitely more threatening : a mixture of feminine dependence ('she-did-it-for-her-man') and of gross inhumanity.

The idea of a woman being involved with the mishandling of children in any way is far worse than a man doing the same thing, because by doing so she denies the sanctity of motherhood. In the public eye, Myra Hindley is a pariah. She symbolises a taboo, and rather than look at what lies behind her undoubtedly chilling case, we take refuge in horrified vindictiveness. When she came up for parole early in 1985 the popular press went berserk. The *Sun* even photographed a relative of one of the murdered children, brandishing a knife – as soon as she got out he would plunge it in her – and splashed it across the front page.

The newspaper reports at the time of the trial were rather more subdued. But even though both Brady and Hindley were charged jointly with murder, it was she who first hit the headlines – 'MOOR TRIAL WOMAN ON MURDER CHARGE' (*Daily Mirror*, April 20, 1966) – a distortion not justified by facts which emerged at the trial, showing him to be the initiator of all the terrible tortures and killings. Anyway, Myra Hindley, 'dressed in a mottle grey suit with a pale blue blouse', charged with the murder of Leslie Ann Downey, ten, and Edward Evans, seventeen, was hardly the stuff of pin-up stereotypes. So the papers played it straight. She has become a 'monster' in the intervening years: the only mould the press can find for her.

One image emphasised by defence counsel at the trial was that of an all-dominant man, Brady, to the younger woman's compliant mistress. 'He dictated to her...' said Godfrey Heilpern, QC, about Myra's secretarial work for Brady, 'and that relationship spilled over into their private affairs.' From comments she made at the trial she certainly *did* seem very scared of Brady, and very much in his power. She acted as unwilling accomplice because she was undoubtedly hooked on him. She says 'I would have done anything so long as Ian did not get into trouble.'

This relationship was transformed into gross sexual titillation by Emlyn Williams in his book, brought out two years after the trial. In *Beyond Belief* he speculates on the first time Ian Brady 'conquered' Myra sexually, and whether 'the brutality of the naked beast above her was mysteriously arousing in her a new and exciting servitude.' Thus out of a complex, highly disturbing case, came cheap pornography, titillating the public, obscuring the facts.

The emotions surrounding the Moors murders ran high in 1966, and women – as mother figures – were deemed particularly susceptible: at the request of the defence the four women on the jury were dismissed, and replaced by men. And the second aspect of Myra's role in the murders was itself tightly bound up with a warped image of motherhood. She was the one to keep little girl Leslie Downey quiet, and calm her down when Brady took photographs, tape recorded or gagged her, for his deathly games. Myra was described as a 'reluctant participant' throughout Brady's antics. And – a significant difference in the two characters – when recordings of the child were played out in court, while Brady just felt 'embarrassed', Myra Hindley confessed, 'I feel *ashamed*'.

Again, Emlyn Williams embellishes these details for his book, playing the amateur psychologist to prove how vilely perverted and confused this woman is. He relates a tale of a holiday tragedy in Myra's childhood, where a friend died in a disused reservoir. He interprets this moment in her life as significant, plunging her, he maintains, into obsessive morbidity. She was, he continues, like a mother who loses her child and suspects 'wicked forces' at work. (Remember, she is still a child herself at this point.) Convinced that 'evil' was being used against her, concludes Williams, using child bearing terms to build up his sick image, 'It lay dormant like a foetus. And like a foetus it grew.'

With blatant nonsense like that, and with the similarly rabid stories that have cropped up regularly since in the popular press, showing the usual haggard police photo of Myra Hindley, twenty years out of date, there is little chance for people to really understand her true involvement in this terrible case. The pain and fury of the children's relatives is completely understandable (though not the way the media capitalises on it). So too is the recent comment from Myra Hindley's mother: 'When they (press and public) call her the Beast and the Devil, they don't know what they are talking about. They don't know her'. (The *Sun*, June 20, 1985) Until she speaks for herself, we will none of us know her. What made her become involved in such a terrible crime? But maybe we don't want break the taboo anyway? She is the monster to keep all *our* monsters well at bay.

An alternative reality: new heroines, real women

Compared with the muddy distortions of reality created by the popular press, the fictional world of television, film, theatre and literature can seem vastly more revealing about women and crime. Sometimes art liberates essential truths. And although each medium has its limitations – its censorship and preconceived ideas – in the same way that Fleet Street does, some vital images are emerging in the 1980s: images which dispense with the mistress/mother/monster syndrome, to concentrate on real women – and bring new heroines to replace those tired old male heroes.

Television

There is no shortage of major parts these days for women in crime series – at least on the 'right' side of the law. Cops and robbers series have certainly changed since I was girl, when *Dixon of Dock Green*, with Dixon, the avuncular British bobby, was staple fare, and not a woman was to be seen, either wearing uniform or making top decisions. Now we have the efficient, effective women inspectors of *Juliet Bravo* and *The Gentle Touch*, and wisecracking female sergeants facing shoot-outs beside male colleagues in the San Franciscan chaos of *Hill Street Blues*. Undercover agents these days travel in *mixed* pairs, with *Dempsey and Makepeace* in Britain – he dark, slow, but strong; she blonde and smartwitted; and *Cover Up* in America – a strange combination of male model Jack and photographer Danielle, 'covering up' as FBI investigators.

These changes are cosmetic. Each programme does something to remind us that women may look and act tough – but underneath they're vulnerable. The very title *Gentle Touch* undermines actress Jill Gascoigne's policewoman authority; Dempsey is forever flirting with Makepeace as he rescues her from a dangerous situation she can't quite handle on her own; Danielle and Jack of *Cover Up* are platonic colleagues – but he did slide into bed with her in one episode, apologetic, but turned on (and the theme tune, Bonnie Tyler's 'Holding Out For A Hero' – 'he's gotta be strong... he's gotta be part of the fight' – carries tell-tale echoes of those macho 'good guys' the series superficially eschews).

One admirable exception to the rule is *Cagney and Lacey* – a series created by two women about a female cop duo who tackle not only the American crime wave, but also the entrenched attitudes of their male counterparts. (One episode even exposed sexual harassment towards Cagney by a superior officer, sensitively and powerfully.) But the super-duo are not immune to pressures of conformity – their clothes were vamped up after early fears that they were rather too 'butch'.

On the other side of the legal divide, 'villainesses' are often portrayed as hard bitches or disaffected punk teenagers; madly menopausal or in the sway of some maniacal lover. Sex is a vital ingredient. One long-running Australian series called *Prisoner* even set itself in a *co-educational* prison, for extra sex appeal. When the inmates were not getting married to each other, then there were checkshirted hints at lesbianism – though when one lesbian character was portrayed as overtly gross and butch, many watchers were perspicacious enough to write in and complain. It didn't happen again.

Occasionally something happens, not just to hint at changing values – as all these series do, albeit in a token, superficial way – but to break the mould dramatically. A series produced in 1983 by Euston Films for ITV, England, did this. It was called *Widows* and was written by Lynda La Plante.

'Much of the pleasure in crime fiction', writes Gillian Skirrow, 'is in its foregrounding of fast and violent action between men.'[10] Lynda La Plante took this same formula with *Widows* and transplanted four women into the leading roles. Dolly, Shirley, Linda and Bella (three of them widowed by a massive bank raid carried out by their husbands – which failed – and the fourth a streetwise black woman, pulled into the action) transform themselves from being submissive helpmates to criminal men, into operating as top-class criminals themselves. They do a second run at the bank raid which killed their men, and they succeed – running off with the loot to foreign parts.

Lynda La Plante was fed up with standard 'villain' programmes, where the woman was always just 'a hooker, somebody's idiot girlfriend, someone who squeals, or a woman in rollers, screaming in the background.' So she took away the safety net of the men – and let the women rip. Unlike the standard male thrillers, the women in *Widows* were credible and real, each woman a recognisable three-dimensional character – from the tough East Ender Dolly to the Italian-born hell-raiser Linda. Despite this touch of realism – or perhaps because of it – television critics were aghast at what *Widows* did. Despite the public barometer of massive ratings to support it, *Widows* was dubbed 'immoral' by male writers in the *Guardian*, the *Financial Times* and the *London Standard*. Why? As Lynda La Plante says: 'You never saw a car chase, you never saw them commit physical violence except for 3½ minutes. They didn't shoot anybody. They didn't fistfight anybody. But they *did* commit a crime.' Women don't do that sort of thing, you see – and if they must, then they must *not* get away with it. . .

The double standard here makes La Plante furious: 'Christ, you've got villains in Spain who've been living there for centuries! Who's screaming about Biggs? He's like a local hero. Cagney portrayed a villain in practically every film he made, but he was a hero – because he shed a few tears.' But the critics got their way. In the follow-up series, two women were killed, one was forced into perpetual exile, and the fourth was arrested. As the author says, 'It does not glamorise crime in any way', but it *was*, as one television magazine succinctly put it, 'an exhilarating punch in the teeth' for popular culture.

Less of a blockbuster than *Widows*, but also offering an unusual slant on crime, was a 1985 BBC series called *Inside Out*. Writer Simon Moore did not pitch for heroines when he showed two ex-prisoners setting up their own employment agency – eschewing the 'narrow ultra-successful band of villains who go round with stockings on their heads shooting banks' of mainstream television, for 'a mass of eccentrics and criminal failures and drop-outs banding together.'

The agency was headed by a stroppy anti-heroine called Carla, a middle-class woman originally inside for drug smuggling, and just as snobby about other criminals as her background would suggest. In one episode, where the agency is catering for a high-class society wedding, she assumes, quite wrongly that her black female colleague is stealing the family silver. Simon Moore is adamant that he wanted 'a character who wasn't a Juliet Bravo, who wasn't ultra-capable but someone who just shouted at people and got herself in a mess.'

But Carla has her strengths and her independence, as well as vulnerabilities. She is a credible character, far more so than the super-good stars in cop cars. Strong women like these on television are still very, very rare – and in order to be truly tough, you still have to be seen as *deviant* in some way. Actress Lou Wakefield, who played Carla, remarked after her two-month television run: 'I think it's rather interesting that there's *Inside Out* and there's *Widows* (in 1983/4/5) and that both are about criminals. Can you name another series where there's a strong woman's part? I can't.'

The tragedy is that despite actresses being successful in three-dimensional roles like these, television casting directors are still scared. When I spoke to Lou Wakefield a couple of months after *Inside Out* finished, she told me that 'although I got exceptional reviews, I've not had an interview for another job.' And Maureen O'Farrell, who gave a brilliant portrayal of Linda in *Widows* told the *TV Times* that 'I have worked only 32 days in the two years since the first series.' In that series she played a young working-class woman – close to her own background – and she insists, in her career, on credible female parts, ones where 'I won't be patronised'. That combination of uncompromising independence in real life, and genuine heroism on the screen, is one too powerful for the conservative bosses of mainstream television. They may try and clamp down, but it will be hard to stem the radical counterflow now it has started.

Theatre

Although western theatre is swinging, 1930s style, towards big-time musicals and mindless farces (to take our minds off the 1980s New Depression), and although the high-kicking, busty images of women here are appallingly reactionary, the non-commercial, grassroots side of theatre is, by its very nature, far more radical and iconoclastic than the mass medium of television.

Work within this medium by a unique British group of ex-prisoners (all women) called Clean Break (see chapter 2) looks specifically at criminal women – their problems and their resilience – and was actually founded in Askham Grange Prison, England, in 1978. The group bases its work on the controversial premise that one reason women turn to crime is to release their frustrated creativity. Says founder member Jenny Hicks, 'You need energy and inventiveness for crime.' But the initial 'high' felt by some women, is soon replaced by the frustration of an even more confining set of stereotypes than those of conventional society. 'When you step outside the law', says Jenny, 'you are forced to play a role,' by police, courts, prisons. Clean Break, as its name suggests, uses the methods of theatre – in workshops and performances – to break this vicious circle in the criminal world, both for performers and spectators.

Their work reaches important sectors like the probation service and community centres, as well as stage and television; and the spectrum of their work is wide: from a youthful, lively show about the 1950s, called *The Easter Egg* (based on the real-life initiation into thieving of author Chris Tchaikovsky), which shows how easy it is for rebellious girls to get hauled up before the courts; to the semi-comic, semi-sombre examination of life on a high security wing for suspected Irish 'terrorist' Judith Ward in *Decade* by Jacki Holborough.

Theatre elsewhere has produced some powerful statements about the political nature of female crime in the last ten years. From Italy, anarchist writers Dario Fo and Franca Rame, in their play *The Fourth Wall*, produced a shocking monologue from German urban guerrilla Ulrike Meinhof, in which she talks about the 'clean white state', shutting her up in prison out of 'fear that you have created not the best of all possible worlds but the worst.'

In America, writer Sharon Pollock has reinterpreted the story of Lizzie Borden in *Blood Relations*. Lizzie Borden axed her stepfather and mother to death in 1892, and Sharon Pollock shows how, conversely, they were killing *her* with deadly restrictions on her life, and how the murders were a last-ditch resort to secure her own survival.

From black Britain, Edgar White offers *Ascension Ritual* which looks at the black youth in London, who are committing crime as a direct and tangible result of white imperialism. Most of his characters are male, but there is also young Sharon, fierce to defend herself outside the stereotypes imposed by white people on the black population – 'It's alright if you can run like (black athlete) Sonia bloody Lansman' – and unrepentant for thieving: 'Sure I stole, but not as much as they (the white British) stole from us.'

And from the British women's movement in 1983 came Sarah Daniels' *Masterpieces*, a polemical attack on pornography in which the soft-hearted liberal heroine becomes aware of how men threaten her on the street – and finally pushes a hustler in front of a train and kills him, in self-defence – and in defiance. Although many women's theatre groups have looked at the broader issues of feminism, this play was remarkable both for reaching a wide audience – taking the main stage of Chelsea's Royal Court Theatre – and for not just showing a serious crime, but showing the defendant up in court at the end –

unrepentant, and even winning a policewoman over to her point of view. The question this play posed was – who, in broad terms, committed the real crime?

Film

Commercial cinema is none too up-to-date about images of women – whether 'deviant' or 'normal'. Criminal women are invariably femmes fatales in the James Bond fashion: black 'tigress' creations, like Grace Jones' villainess in 007's *A View To Kill*, and Tina Turner's half-crazed demon figure in *Mad Max, Beyond Thunderdome* and drug pusher Acid Queen in *Tommy* are particularly popular. Or they are simply seen as imitation men. The British movie *Scum*, about boys in borstal, was complemented later by Mai Zetterling's female *Scrubbers* which, albeit challenging, did, as its like-sounding title suggests, take the the male prototype from which to work.

It is Holland and Germany which have broken the conventional mould most successfully to give us provocative, radical films about women and crime. *A Question of Silence* by Dutch film-maker Marlene Gorris provoked outraged accusations of 'Stalinist feminism' from British Sunday papers in 1984, because it looked at the politics of female crime – depicting the beating to death of a shop manager by a group of women, after he finds one of them stealing clothes – and because it showed women being violent. As in *Widows*, the killing scene uses minimal shock tactics. What is striking is the women's *rebellion*, a rebellion understood by female spectators, if not the male ones. In Britain cinema audiences were often divided clean down the middle, sex-wise, in their understanding of the startling final scene – where the woman's trial ends in disrespect for male laws, and in female anarchy.

In Germany, Margaretta Von Trotta's first feature, *The Second Awakening Of Christa Klages*, had a theme she developed in later work. It starred a woman on the run from a bank robbery, showed how she coped as a complete 'outsider' to mainstream society, and ended with her finding support from a woman friend in Portugal. Von Trotta's work moved towards more overtly political crime in *The German*

Sisters, analysing the tortured relationship between a feminist journalist and her 'terrorist' sister who was based on the character of Gudrun Ensslin of the West German Red Army Faction.

Each of Von Trotta's films is founded on the basic theme of sisterhood between women, even when their circumstances and convictions seem to preclude that togetherness. Two separate features by Australian and American women also move with this theme, carrying overtly political messages. The first, *On Guard*, is about four women who sabotage a research programme into reproductive engineering planned by a multi-national firm, and the second, *Born In Flames*, directed by Lizzie Borden (who renamed herself in honour of the nineteenth-century killer featured in Sharon Pollock's play) shows the armed takeover by a group of black and white women of a television and radio network.

All these films are a mixture of romantic heroism and a serious projection of what might happen if women stopped complying with their perceived role in western society – and started using 'criminal' methods to make a political point about their particular oppression.

On a more immediately realistic level, the cinema image of women and crime has been radically challenged by Mike Newell's consummately skilful film *Dance with a Stranger*, discussed earlier in the chapter. The script, by Shelagh Delaney, shows how far the popular image of Ruth Ellis, as the free-fucking, working-class tart, and David Blakely, as the gentrified nob who could not escape her wicked clutches, deviates from what probably happened.

In the film, when Blakely swears he'll have no peace till she marries him, Ruth says, 'I've *never* had any peace.' When he castigates her for sleeping with other men, saying, 'Some people have no shame', she is swift to reply, 'Some people have enough for everyone.' This is a neat inversion of class moralism and a subtle preparation for her final action, with its devastating consequences. It is as far from James Bond artificial chic as you could possibly get.

Literature

Fantasy crime fiction has always had a strong female input – with women like Agatha Christie, Patricia Highsmith, P.D. James and Ruth Rendell leading the field of detective/thriller writers. But they are fairly reactionary about their own sex, perpetuating some of the more unfortuante stereotypes via the characters they describe. This is a classic comment from Detective Dalgliesh, in P.D. James' *Unnatural Causes*, about Lil, a prime suspect in a nasty murder case: 'Lil, Dalgliesh remembered, was like most women. She lied most effectively when she could convince herself that, essentially, she was telling the truth.'

But since the 1970s, radical writers have also taken up the thriller genre, giving it a more biting feminist edge. Murder, just as in Victorian times, remains the favourite criminal topic. In *Murder In The English Department* by Valerie Miner, an English professor, Angus Murchie, is stabbed by a beautiful woman student whom he had been sexually harassing; in *Here Today* by Zoe Fairbairns, a working-class typing temp avenges a similar crime; and in *Killing Wonder* by Dorothy Bryant, a whole pile of women suspects are gathered before the corpse of India Wonder, big-time writer they all adored – and all might have murdered.

Some modern fiction deliberately tips the balance *away* from male heroes, to female ones. And television writer Simon Moore reckons that 'We've had fantasy heroes for a long time who are men, so it seems absolutely right to me that we should have fantasy heroines.' Two recent novels really encourage the dreamers. *Any Four Women Could Rob the Bank of Italy* by Ann Cornelisen[11] is based on the sexism of Italian police. Cornelisen's ironic theory is that they are so incapable of seeing women as anything but decoration that any women could commit, and get away with, a large-scale robbery. Give the police an accurate description of four women, says Cornelisen, and they would still go off hunting for four men! So... El, Lacey, Hermione, and Caroline turn the Great Train Robbery of the 1960s into the Great Tuscan Train Robbery of the 1980s! The crime is never solved, the case closed. In the closing paragraph of the book, El remembers 'an intriguing article about the Vatican Bank. Nuns are the truly invisible women: priests never notice them, much less the police. Now if...'

From heroines of the present to heroines of the distant past. *Moll*

Cutpurse[12] by Ellen Galford is a fabulous rewrite of history, taking the real-life character of 'roaring madcap Moll', an Elizabethan thief, cutpurse and swaggerer – 'deep-eyed and well-pickled in sin' – and pursuing her *true* story (not the sanitised version of Middleton and Dekker who first celebrated this rogue in *The Roaring Girl*). Pipe-smoking, breech-wearing Moll fairly rips around the countryside, opening a College for Young Pickpockets, challenging the Puritan backlash with 'blaspheming and riotous behaviour' and ending her days in more stately fashion, as 'a kind of mother magistrate to the underworld'.

But when the fun stops and the real modern world looms large, where are the books with authentic experiences of women who have crossed the line into crime? There are plenty of sociological terms dating back to the nineteenth century – some useful, many not – which look *at* criminal women, but precious few *by* them. We do not yet have anything to match the full-length accounts of men such as Jimmy Boyle, whose *A Sense of Freedom* and *The Pain of Confinement* cover both his crime-filled early life and his years inside. Although there *are* books, like *A Woman in Custody*,[13] which deal specifically with the prison end of female crime, these give only a partial and victim's view of the whole picture.

Some books do work to fill this gap. *Criminal Women*[14] carries short autobiographical accounts by four women, including one on the youthful anarchy of Chris Tchaikovsky, whose early thieving was inspired by Camus' dictum that 'in every act of rebellion one is being true to a part of oneself'; and one which reveals the complexity of Diana Christina – whose social and sexual repression changed her from 'the young, comfortably-off girl educated at the French Lycée in London' to 'the prostitute, the cat burglar, the shoplifter, the pimp...'

Nancy Spungen, who sprang to notoriety through her ill-fated affair with Sex Pistol Sid Vicious, and was finally stabbed to death by him, suffered a particularly ferocious hate campaign by the media in the late 1970s. Now the story behind the slogans – *And I Don't Want to Live This Life*[15] has been told by her mother Deborah Spungen, who gives details of her daughter's troubled life – the stealing, the drugs, the schizophrenia, but also the intelligence and frustrated compassion – and shows how Nancy's 'deviant' life was distorted by popular myth. 'Nancy died with a knife in her stomach, the whole world there to gape at her... The press called her Nauseating Nancy... In life the media had made my daughter into a distasteful celebrity; in death, they made her a freak.' *And I Don't Want to Live This Life* uncovers the pain behind the freakshow.

In *Woman At Point Zero*[16] (see chapter 1) Nawal El Saadawi issues a more wide-ranging and more cutting political statement, with its extraordinary, true story of Firdaus, an Egyptian prostitute hanged in 1973 for killing her pimp. El Saadawi met Firdaus on Death Row and was immediately struck by her calm and integrity: 'It looked to me as though this woman who had killed a human being and was shortly to be killed herself, was a much better person than I.'

Slowly, Firdaus tells her story: of an impoverished childhood, and enforced marriage in Cairo to the 60-year-old Sheikh Mahmoud; of 'escape' into prostitution as the only means she can find to be independent, and then of work in a big industrial firm – where all the women provide slave labour and where she realises that 'a successful prostitute was better than a misled saint'; of entrapment by a powerful pimp Marzouk, who controls a network not only of women prostitutes, but also of doctors, police and court officials; and of her ultimate revenge – his stabbing. 'I knew I hated him as only a woman can hate a man; as only a slave can hate a master.' She then tells a rich client what she has done. The police are called. Calmly, she says to them, 'I am a killer, but I've committed no crime. Like you, I kill only criminals.' Who *are* the real criminals, asks Firdaus? Any men who subjugate, humiliate, and terrorise women. 'When I killed', she says, 'I did it with truth, not with a knife.' What we need now is more of that truth – however unpalatable it may prove to be, and however challenging to our traditional, comforting, but desperately misleading ideas about what *makes* a woman – and about what makes that woman commit crime.

CHAPTER 6

THE POLITICAL CONNECTION

History was a sense of urgency, a rush in the blood and a passion to make things better, to push with her whole life on what was. (Heroine of Marge Piercy's *Vida*, Women's Press, 1980)

There is a distinct and qualitative difference between breaking a law for one's own individual self interest and violating it in the interests of a class or a people whose oppression is particularised through that law. The former might be called criminal (though in many ways s/he is a victim), but the latter, as a reformist or revolutionary, is interested in universal social change. Captured, he or she is a political prisoner. (Angela Davis, *If They Come in the Morning*, Orbach & Chambers, 1971)

I don't know about this word 'political'. I think it's very divisive in prison and I think it's wrong. We are all political prisoners, or we are *not* political prisoners. It's one or the other. You're all there for different reasons, but you've all broken the law to get there. (Jenny Hicks)

A sharp divide is usually made, in public discussions about crime, between the legal offence of an individual or private group, and the 'political crime' of women committed to a particular radical organisation or ideology – women who break a law to change the world. The 'ordinary criminal' and the 'political prisoner' are rarely considered to have anything in common. Books on criminology often steer clear of subjects like political bombings or demonstrations – and also avoid the political implicatons of everyday crimes in the street. But there are links and divisions between these different actions which need to be examined. If women's crime can be seen, in some respects, as a form of rebellion – against poverty or powerlessness or female conditioning – then some 'political crime' is not entirely dissimilar in its underlying motives. There are women political prisoners all over the world, as Amnesty International will affirm – and they suffer as much abuse as do criminalised women, with frightening labels like 'terrorist' to stigmatise them. (Even a harmless and accurate term, such as 'Greenham Common woman', used to describe the peace campaigners at the American nuclear air base in Berkshire, has *itself* become a scaremongering derogatory phrase in the media, during the history of the camp.) But often these women are held, and keep themselves, quite apart from other prisoners. Their status is different. Why? What *is* 'political crime'? Who are some of its practitioners? What are their aims? And can they really be reconciled with the women who thieve, who prostitute themselves, who kill their husbands; those who commit crime to *survive*, as well as to protest?

DEFINITIONS

'Political crime' is offically defined in the *Dictionary of Criminology*, in reference to one-party states and dictatorships; authors Walsh and Poole specifically mention the Soviet Union and Latin America, where 'thousands have been killed or have suffered long incarceration *for holding beliefs or opinions considered dangerous or undesirable by the authorities*.[1] Even that can be a political 'crime'. But of course it is not just official dictatorships who operate like this. The West does it too Black American activist Claudia Jones, who campaigned for civil rights in the USA, in the 1940s and 1950s witnessed the arrest of many friends and colleagues during the vicious McCarthy witchhunts of the time. Arrest for what? 'For the crime of holding independent political ideas.'[2] Many people in Northern Ireland tell a similar story of 'Crime by association', of being arrested as suspects connected to the outlawed Irish Republican Army, through family, or simply Catholic, allegiances.

There are, in addition, women who do not simply espouse political ideals, but who commit illegal, sometimes violent acts in support of them: whether peacefully occupying nuclear bases in Britain (like the Greenham Common campaigners) or – at the most extreme and militant end of the political spectrum – kidnapping top military and business men (like the Red Army Faction in West Germany); bombing military targets (like the IRA in Northern Ireland and Britain); and carrying out armed bank raids to raise funds for their groups (like the Symbionese Liberation Army and related groups in the USA). The latter are dismissed as 'terrorists' by the governments who fight them, in an effort to undermine their power and influence, and Walsh and Poole endorse this official view when they state quite categorically that 'Terrorism is characteristically a weapon of the weak pretending to be strong'. But, as they go on to say, 'terrorism' is also being misused increasingly as an easy way of defusing *any* political threat – such as guerrilla warfare in places like South Africa. Whatever your opinion about activists involved in these conflicts (see 'The call to arms', this chapter), their impetus to act is definitely political; their fought-for status, when arrested, that of 'political prisoner'.

Patti Hearst was one of the most controversial American 'guerrilla converts' of recent years, remarkable mainly for her switch from kidnap victim to rebel supporter of her kidnappers. She is the daughter of US newspaper tycoon Randolph Hearst, and was taken captive in the early 1970s by an organisation called the Symbionese Liberation Army – 'symbiosis' implying racial and sexual interdependence, and the forging of links between different left-wing groups. Set up initially to protest against the Vietnam War, the SLA mounted a wave of guerrilla actions in the early 1970s. Patti joined forces with them while under kidnap, and proved of useful propaganda value in transmitting messages to the press (her father's newspapers), in which she linked the SLA to the IRA and others, and called them all 'ideological soldiers'.

One of the SLA's demands was a free food programme for America's poor, and a six million dollar ransom for Patti. But she became one of them, and even took an active part in a daring armed bank raid by the group. In a public statement after the raid she gave her own definition of what had happened, and also of what constitutes a political crime: 'our action forced the corporate state to help finance the revolution. In the case of expropriation, the difference between a criminal act and a revolutionary act is shown by what the money is used for.'[3] She implies by this that the SLA used their funds for the greater good of oppressed people, rather than for individual consumption. (Like so many underground organisations, spawned amid the radical flowering of the 1960s, the SLA has since disappeared. Patti herself has served her sentence, and is married.)

Angela Davis gives a similar analysis to Patti Hearst, built on socialist rhetoric, and rather dismissive of the 'non-political' crime: 'The majority of criminal offences bear a direct relationship to property... This type of crime is at once a protest against society and a desire to partake of its exploitative content. It challenges the symptoms of capitalism but not its essence.'[4] Political action, she maintains, in contrast, *does* challenge this 'essence' although not always with a high degree of success, and is thereby given a loftier status: its own morality.

Militant feminists have also justified the use of illegal actions for their own particular philosophy: outright opposition to the consistent use of sexual violence by men against women. Where the ideals and political definitions of socialists like Angela Davis are based on race and class, radical feminists make divisions on the grounds of sex and gender. They have opposed the deliberate effort made by many men, both verbally and physically, to make women feel inferior, and their retaliation has in some cases been dramatic. In 1968 Valerie Solanas shot and wounded pop artist Andy Warhol, in protest at his pornographic images of women. She also published something called the SCUM Manifesto, in which she urged women to 'stop buying, just loot, and simply refuse to obey all laws (you) don't care to obey'.[5] Laws, she maintained, were made *by* men and *for* them. As such, women had no place obeying them!

Similar militancy prevailed in Britain in 1980, when a mass rapist, Peter Sutcliffe, was terrorising women in the Leeds area. In response both to the threat posed by him, and to a bout of violent films issued at the time, like *Dressed to Kill*, *The Shining*, and *The Violation of the Bitch (She Asked For It)*, a pressure group called Women Against Violence Against Women (WAVAW) was set up, to organise mass demonstrations in places like Soho, London's porn centre. Another group, called Angry Women, initiated several direct attacks against cinemas and sex shops. Here is a public statement from Angry Women in 1980: 'In Greater Manchester women have disrupted films which glorify the exploitation of women, and present sadism as entertainment. We have glued the locks of shops which make money from selling degrading images of women. We have destroyed magazines which show us as things to be used by men.' In February 1981 a sex shop was burned in Chapeltown, Leeds, causing £3,000 worth of damage: an action claimed by Angry Women.

What justifies this kind of action? How is a judge to decide whether it is a just political protest, or wilful criminal damage? In cases like this, the defendant relies on legal advocates understanding the intention behind an act of rebellion – an intention not always in line with the ethics of the system they represent. Amazingly, sometimes they do. Veteran activist Pat Arrowsmith remembers, 'There was one incident where I smashed a disgusting pornographic clock on sale in Covent Garden and the security guards did a citizen's arrest of me. It was *so* pornographic – exposing women's genitalia – that I got an absolute discharge.' Here, politics completely overruled the crime.

PEACEFUL PROTESTS

Political defiance of the law is by no means always linked with militant or aggressive action. In fact one of the most effective women's campaigns of the early 1980s in Europe has been the anti-nuclear movement initiated at Greenham Common, Berkshire.

In 1981 a group of protestors called 'Women For Life On Earth' left Cardiff to march to Greenham Common, an American airforce base which was due to house Cruise missiles, first-strike nuclear weapons, in 1983. An all-woman peace camp was set up out of this initial action, making repeated protests inside and outside the camp, and attracting massive media publicity. In December 1982 30,000 women arrived to encircle the base. In December 1983, the year of the Cruise missiles' arrival, the number increased to 50,000. Meanwhile a core of women camped constantly, through conditions of cold and hardship, risking arrest and harassment at all times. The imaginative and unrelenting activities of the women at Greenham – naming each of the camp's gates with a colour, decorating the fences with toys and colourful peace symbols, spinning webs of wool round each other and round the base, dressing as witches and symbolically sweeping away the danger with their brooms – captured the curiosity and interest of the world. Although the media has long since lost affection for Greenham, the camp still goes on; women break into the base regularly to draw attention to police and military rule; and protestors clog up the courts with their lengthy defence pleas – which officers of the law are forced to hear and absorb. Their use of the legal system is ingenious – when some of them were charged with breach of the peace, they quoted the 1969 Genocide Act, which prohibits the physical destruction of group life anywhere. Cruise, they argued, could easily wipe out the whole of Europe. About one thing they are absolutely clear: we each have a profound responsibility to stop the nuclear threat. 'It is individuals who make the silos... and individuals who drag women away to police cells.'[6] It is also individuals who sit down and blockade the road; who cut through barbed wire fences and dance on the silos, who brave the jeers, taunts and physical bullying of soldiers; individual women who through action become unified.

Greenham is the flowering of an anti-nuclear movement which was forged in Britain in the 1950s and '60s: a movement which first focussed on the Aldermaston marches, and whose participants incurred the same rough treatment from the authorities as today. Pat Arrowsmith has been a famous and tireless anti-war campaigner: her experiences range from being dumped in an ice-cold pond by drunk construction workers at a Norfolk missile site in 1958, to serving sentences for anti-Vietnam activities, and for leafletting the troops in Northern Ireland – incurring legal wrath for such grandiose charges as 'incitement to mutiny' along the way! She has been inside prison ten times.

But her quality of fearlessness and tenacity stands out. She is a woman prepared to act. She says: 'It's the action you take that's important, rather than the consequences.' That kind of moral imperative informs much of the peace movement – the need, as Lorraine and Helen, both Greenham women, explained, to do something concrete. They remember a recent incident: 'There were all these holes in the fence, made by other women and then left – and before we could stop and rationalise what was happening we were inside. It was an emotional decision, made extremely quickly.' Result: arrest. Mission successful. A quiet determination to see protest through to its logical conclusion.

THE CALL TO ARMS

I love people
love nature
love love
I am a revolutionary
nothing special
one soul
one life willing

to give it.
Ready to die

(A prison poem by Ericka Huggins, Black Panther)

Much more controversial than the peaceful politics of Greenham – which in many ways can confirm traditional views of women as harmonious and nurturing beings, creating love while the men make war – are the armed revolutionaries who stand *beside* men in violent struggle around the world. What makes a woman become a 'guerrilla': a 'terrorist'? How can she reconcile the conventional machismo of most men in this role with her own need to effect change? The actions of a female 'terrorist' are fraught with contradictions.

In some countries, for example, South Africa and in Latin America, guerrilla warfare is an immediate, essential struggle against an extreme right-wing government. Here, the pragmatic struggle to stay alive and to attain some form of personal liberty is unequivocal. There is no time for arguments about arms. It is kill or be killed. Sometimes such concentrated action is successful, as in Nicaragua, where a people's government was formed in 1979, and is maintained, despite American military incursions via Honduras aimed at destabilisation of the regime. Here there is no talk about whether or not women should fight, or whether the action is politically correct. It is a fight for survival. As one Nicaraguan guerrilla, Gloria, says, 'The tasks of women and the revolution are one and the same.'

But urban guerrilla struggles in Europe are far more ambiguous. British troops currently occupy the streets of Northern Ireland, as a symbol of the centuries-old fight to maintain British rule over Ireland. Sinn Fein ('Ourselves Alone'), the Republican party of the North, and its armed wing, the IRA, which is responsible for strategic bombing of military and government targets in Ulster and mainland Britain, is the symbol of opposition to this rule. Women are closely involved in the North's nationalist struggle – but there are strange contradictions, due to the combined ethics of nationalism and catholicism behind Sinn Fein, which can often still convey a traditional home-and-family attitude towards women. The IRA's military organisation is aggressive and very 'male' in its organising, and action. To be involved, women supporters must to a certain extent put their own feminist liberation into the background, in support of a wider, national liberation – still controlled and led by men.

Urban guerrillas like those of the Red Army Faction in West Germany in the 1970s had something far less immediately tangible to fight for, than the IRA – and their more remote aims, combined with Draconian state measures against them, eventually led to lack of impetus and isolation. They were formed in the early 1970s, influenced, like so many other radical groups, by the anti-Vietnam War movement. They then went underground in the face of the government backlash against radicals, and in order to start a series of kidnaps, murders and bombings. Their esoteric, and inflammatory aim was to undermine the capitalist state by forcing its 'latent fascism' into the open, and then destroying it completely, to make way for revolutionary socialism. In the former they succeeded. Strict measures were brought in, to punish any sympathisers ('Sympathisanten') with the RAF. Intellectuals and radicals were subjected to a virtual witchhunt throughout the 1970s, and the German magazine *Tempo* (February 1986) remembers that 'Society and state reacted like the fighters themselves: explosively, hysterically, with an insatiable greed for enemy targets'. But in the latter, they had less success. The West German state remains intact – more reactionary than ever.

Throughout their campaign, the RAF stressed support for all other liberation struggles, making links in particular with Arab organisations. One of their most spectacular actions was the hijacking of a Lufthansa Boeing to Mogadishu, Somalia, in October 1977. During the action they demanded the release of all German political prisoners including leading RAF figures, Gudrun Ensslin, Andreas Baader and Jan Carl Raspe. The hijack failed – and the three prisoners were found dead in their cells in Stammheim jail next day. Group suicide or state killing? No-one has been allowed to find out...

The significant thing about the RAF is that, unlike many armed struggles, including the IRA, women always played a leading role in its development. Two of its founder members were Ulrike Meinhof and Gudrun Ensslin, both intellectual revolutionaries and committed fighters. There has been a concerted effort by the German gutter press to undermine the importance of these women, by caricaturing their zeal, and suggesting mental instability as a reason for their going underground. Sound familiar? (see chapter 4.) Gudrun in particular has been portrayed in the sensationalist *Hitler's Children* (Granada, 1978) as an 'intense, shrill-voiced' hysteric, who was easily influenced by the 'swaggering, aggressive, domineering' Andreas Baader, who, Jillian Becker would have us believe, completely controlled the women he worked with, and dominated the organisation. The author cannot deny reports of contemporaries, however, who found much charisma and power in the women RAF members. Ulrike seemed especially influential. One of her fellow radicals remembers: 'She conveyed a sense of daring, of rebellion, of risk; of being for things that our parents and most of the world were probably against'.[7] Nonetheless, the RAF was brutal, and rigid in its regime, running its underground cells with masculine hierarchy and discipline, and toting guns with an open commitment to creating 'terror'. While there is something undoubtedly thrilling about a woman daring to flout convention in this way – breaking state laws with an undisguised arrogance, and with contempt for the consequences – it is also very chilling and disconcerting. Her aggressive action, which in one way is so rebellious, is in another way a complete capitulation to age-old methods of working. The man's way. Nonetheless, although in direct opposition to the totally peaceful methods of the Greenham women, and although her advocacy of violence can have dubious repercussions, the urban guerrilla does share two things with other political activists: courage and conviction.

PRISON PARADOXES: THE FIGHT FOR POLITICAL STATUS

'I saw her walk out with them. I never saw her again. But her voice continued to echo in my ears, vibrating in my head, in the cell, in the prison, in the streets, in the whole world, shaking everything, spreading fear wherever it went, the fear of the truth which kills, the power of truth, as savage, and as simple, and as awesome as death, yet as simple and as gentle as the child that has not yet learnt to lie.

'And because the world was full of lies, she had to pay the price.'[8]

Nawal El Saadawi writes here about the Arab woman called Firdaus, a prostitute who kills her pimp out of a deep rooted, *political* hatred of all the men who have abused her, and of the male system itself. Firdaus is introduced to the author as someone suffering from 'mental affliction' (a label often used by regimes to dismiss any kind of dissident). But El Saadawi soon sees that she is nothing of the kind, but 'a woman apart'. Firdaus has the conviction of her beliefs – her hatred of absolute repression, and her faith in absolute justice. 'Firdaus', says the author, 'is the story of a woman driven by despair to the darkest of ends. This woman, despite her misery and despair, evoked in all those who, like me, witnessed the final moments of her life, a need to challenge and overcome those forces that deprive human beings of their right to live, to love and to real freedom.' Firdaus is hanged. But to the last she retains her dignity, tenacity and inner calm. She is the essence of a political prisoner.

Like Firdaus, Greenham women carry the same pride and dignity to their trials, often using the courtroom to make a political point: 'I do not feel I stand here today as a criminal. I feel this court is dealing in trivia by making this charge against us, while those who are the real criminals (those who deal in our deaths) continue their conspiracy against humankind. The law is concerned with property. We are concerned with the preservation of all life. How dare the government presume the right to kill others in our name?' (Statement to Newbury Magistrates Court, April 14, 1982) For these women, arrest and imprisonment is all part of the protest...

The turn of the screw

Prisoners of conscience suffer some of the worst torment and deprivation known to humanity. The payment for dissenting in words or action, against state power, can be anything from withdrawal of food, exercise and health care, to hard labour, sensory deprivation, beatings, rape, torture and death. Laws are bent, broken, or changed in order to incarcerate political activists, or even sympathisers. At the time of the RAF bombings and kidnappings in West Germany, eminent writers like Heinrich Böll were harassed, their families' homes turned over, if they so much as spoke about the RAF in terms less than baldly condemnatory. To be 'Sympathisant' – someone who understood or supported the RAF's ideals and aims, if not their methods – was almost as bad as being an actual guerrilla, in the eyes of the government. In Northern Ireland similar things happen. One woman's father and family were hounded by the police; she was arrested when she was sixteen, and has been picked up regularly since: 'Your guilt is not established at your trial. Mine was established at birth. I was Catholic, and worse, I was Republican.'[9]

In 1976 the London Labour government attempted to intensify the struggles of the Republicans, and to criminalise Irish prisoners locked up for Republican activities, by removing the Special Category Status which gave them certain rights, and tacitly acknowledged their political presence. This process was called variously 'criminalisation', 'Ulsterisation', and ironically 'normalisation'. All it did was precipitate highly publicised protests – hunger strikes and the no-wash campaigns, by the prisoners, who simply refused to accept the attempt to silence them. Normal legal procedures are now circumvented in Northern Ireland by the Emergency Provisions Act, which allows trial without a jury (in the so-called Diplock Courts), minimal bail, powers to arrest without a warrant, and admissibility of confessed evidence. 'Confessions' are elicited at a special interrogation centre, Castlereagh. Further convictions are secured by the infamous 'supergrass' system, where paid informers are trained to give lists of names, and people are convicted on the shaky word of one man. Add to this the use of long remands to keep suspects under jurisdiction –

and you have an effective, stringent regime, based on a bedrock of harassment and humiliation.

Angela Davis remembers similar aggravation for black activists in America. When Civil Rights leader Martin Luther King was arrested, she says, he was never charged with breaching the peace, etc, but with being 'an enemy of the state': a nebulous term, and with frightening implications, as prophesied in George Orwell's *1984*, where people could be charged with *thoughtcrime* – the penalty for having even a thought which contradicts state policy! Ericka Huggins, a Black Panther leader, was falsely charged with conspiracy to murder another Panther. In this case, the judge dismissed the charge. Angela Davis herself was arrested for conspiracy in 1970 for the Marin County Court hold-up by Jonathan Jackson. She was picked up through her political activities and her support of George and Jonathan Jackson – the Soledad Brothers – on other occasions. Again, this was guilt by association, and an overt injustice which attracted worldwide criticism.

There is extra menace for political prisoners once they are convicted and sent down. The staff are sometimes primed to exert maximum severity and force, and they may even harbour personal grievances (if they have a relative who has been a victim of political bombings, for example). This is aggravated still further by periodic clampdowns on prisoners by the authorities, again as a means of political retaliation. In 1982, in Northern Ireland, Murtagh became the new governor of Armagh women's jail. This followed shortly after the hunger strike by prisoners, which had received international publicity, and had greatly helped the Republican cause. Suddenly a campaign of petty harassment of prisoners was instigated. Women would be put into solitary for things like switching the television channel over without permission. They also began to be stripsearched with alarming frequency. This procedure is carried out on a very wide basis throughout Britain as well as Ireland, and both political and 'non-political' prisoners suffer its indignities. The rationale behind it is that women could conceal things – drugs, messages, etc. – inside their body orifices, while out in court, or on transfer to another jail. So each time the prisoner leaves the prison, and each time she returns, she is made to strip naked, and to turn round in front of an officer. It is an extremely humiliating experience for all women, and Republican women claim that is it carried out on them to an extreme degree – constituting sexual harassment. The London Armagh Women's Group, which was set up in 1980 after a delegation of women were arrested while protesting outside Armagh jail on International Women's Day, 1979, already makes reference to this practice pre-1982: 'The women are imprisoned because they denied the British government the right to invade their country. For their audacity that same government has sought to invade both their bodies (stripsearching) and their minds.'

The London Armagh Women's Group say that the women are subjected to strip searches in the North far more than the men, and on occasions when it is clearly unnecessary – on remand visits to court, when they never leave the side of a prison officer, and for one woman, even after a visit to the toilet within the prison! Linda Quigley, released from Armagh in 1984: 'There is nothing in a stripsearch only degradation and humiliation. The British Government claim that this is happening for reasons of security. It's not. It's just to degrade and humiliate the woman. That's simply what it's there for.' Briege Ann McCaughey,[10] sentenced to seven years in Armagh, remembers: 'A republican woman had to go to hospital but she was told that before she went she would be stripsearched. So she refused. Another girl, an ordinary prisoner, who had to go to hospital, now that wee girl was not stripsearched. Ordinary prisoners, in for criminal offences, are stripsearched but not as often. We think they are stripsearched only so that no-one can say there is discrimination.'[10]

The *Irish Feminist Review 1984* carried details of particularly gruelling experiences which women who were stripsearched went through. One woman was forced, four weeks after giving birth, to remove both breast pads and sanitary towel. When she put her hands up to stop the milk flowing, she was ordered to put them back by her side. She was still bleeding from the birth, but had no way to stop the blood streaming down her legs. Seven warders were present to witness this. Briege Ann McCaughey is sure that 'the only reason why stripsearching has been introduced is to break the spirit of the Republican women.'[11] But another woman, who was stripsearched in front of eight officers, although feeling 'violated, invaded, victimized.

And very, very angry', underlined the determination of the prisoners not to capitulate: 'I thought of all the women striving everywhere to achieve their freedom... I saw my nakedness as an indictment against them. They thought my womanhood would serve to help defeat me. They didn't understand that the strength of ideals cannot be stripped from one's mind'.[12]

A political prisoner has potential enemies even among those supposed to offer help. In *Kiss of the Spiderwoman* by Manuel Puig, a strange novel about the relationship between two prisoners in a Latin American jail, situations which many women also go through are described, Molina becomes ill, and yet resists seeing the doctor – 'A political prisoner can't afford to end up in an infirmary, ever, you understand?'[13] Doctors, he explains, will give him Seconal, induce an addiction, soften him up and get him to talk. This is one of the most horrifying facts – that healers are used on prisoners to *create* illness. They also use the false label of mental illness – most notably in the Soviet Union, where dissidents are sent to psychiatric hospitals, their views discredited by the 'mad' tag. It happens in Britain too. When Pat Arrowsmith was in prison in Scotland following an anti-Polaris (nuclear submarine) demonstraton, she was confined to solitary for refusing to fill sand bags for civil defence purposes, as part of her prison work. She then went on hunger strike. At one point the governor had 'a word' with her, and gently suggested that she was a little 'muddled' and should see a psychiatrist. Luckily the doctor she saw turned out to be politically sympathetic. He pronounced her completely sane.

In *Kiss of the Spiderwoman*, government tactics also backfire. The prison doctor is appalled at the torture of Molina and gives him unauthorised painkillers: 'The way they've worked you over is unbelievable. Those burns in the groin... It will take weeks to heal up. But don't tell about this or I'm finished.'[14] Valentin, Molina's transvestite cell mate, has been put there on charges of corrupting minors. The regime assumes, homophobically, that he is 'soft', and can be bribed into extracting secrets from Molina. Unfortunately for them, Valentin is actually won over to Molina's cause. He dies carrying out a mission for the revolution.

In Britain we defuse the power of artists and poets by ignoring them. In the Soviet Union they arrest them as subversives. Irina Ratushinskaya was one such writer. One of her friends has written: 'No matter how dreadful it may be to say it, I believe that for a poet in our country to be arrested is a compliment. A peculiar form of recognition for her services to the motherland.' (*City Limits*, May 22, 1986) In September 1982 Irina was arrested and charged with 'agitation carried on for the purpose of subverting or weakening the Soviet regime'. This 'agitation' was human rights activity, and 'preparing and distributing her poems'. She was subsequently imprisoned in Zone Four of Corrective Labour Colony Number Three at Barashevo in Mordovia, along with nine other women prisoners of conscience. One of the others, Natalya Lazareva, has been imprisoned twice for compiling and sending abroad feminist literature. (She allegedly compiled the samizdat *Woman and Russia*, published in English by Sheba.) Feminists, like poets, are dangerous activists to the Soviet state: activists for free speech.

Irina's detention centre, Corrective Labour Colony Number Three, is a hard place. The women work an eight-hour day, making gloves, and face a variety of punishments for failing to meet designated work targets. The worst one is 'shizo' – detention for up to fifteen days in an intensely cold isolation cell. Poor diets, together with frequent hunger strikes, have led to appallingly bad health among the women. Irina herself developed kidney disease. Her life was in danger several times before she was finally released in October 1986.

Often it is the less obviously barbaric practices used against political prisoners which have the more devastating effects. One of the most notorious tortures is sensory deprivation – the removal of all normal conditions of light, touch, movement and sound. The prisoner is denied all contact with the changing time, all connection with the physical world. Pat Arrowsmith, who works for Amnesty International, says, 'there are more unpleasant sequals to sensory deprivation than to the most violent physical torture'.

RAF member Astrid Proll suffered four and a half months of this treatment. She became so ill that doctors warned she would die if she stayed in prison. Ulrike Meinhof, also of the RAF, described sensory deprivation vividly (as recorded by Franca Rame, playwright) as 'the feeling that one's spine is drilling into the brain, that one is pissing one's soul away'. In Margaretta von Trotta's film *The German Sisters*, the repressive regime of Stammheim prison is recreated: the armed guards with Alsatians; the searchlights; the barbed wire and double walls; the massively thick panes of glass between prisoner and visitor; and the microphones which distort conversation, and are switched on and off abruptly, making the inmate feel more confused and alone than she did before the visit.

Stammheim was capable of barbarisms. Three RAF members died simultaneously in October 1977 in their cells (mass suicide, or murder?) and Irmgard Möller claimed she was attacked on the same night with a blunt kitchen knife. At Stammheim crude torture is coupled with the sophisticated electronic perversions which long ago replaced the simple insanity-inducing water drip.

These attacks do not go unchallenged. However much money, manpower and machinery goes into repressing political prisoners – and women prisoners connected with the Irish struggle go through particularly heavy treatment on the British mainland, in places like Durham Jail H Wing (a place thought too extreme for male inmates and now housing only women!) – their idealism and strength of mind dictates exactly the same amount of resistance. When Special Status was taken away from Irish prisoners in 1976 they refused to wear prison clothes, and went 'on the blanket'; 'I'll wear no convict uniform, nor meekly serve my time/That Britain might brand Ireland's fight/800 years of crime' (H Block song). As a continuation of this, the Armagh women went on work strike, and started a no-wash protest. Ten men in H Block later died on hunger strike. The women keep up their morale and steadfastness by keeping an army discipline, with a commanding officer who negotiates between them and the prison authorities. Says the London Armagh Women's Group, 'They are fighting in a war, and they are disciplined political prisoners.' The no-wash protest was a particular hardship for the women – having not just shit, but blood to contend with. But even the filth was transformed into defiance. Margaretta D'Arcy, who took part in the protest: 'All through history tiny bands of rebellious troops had thus proclaimed their pride within stone walls, barbed wire, stockades, and the boundaries of lands of exile. For this lay in excrement, urine, and menstrual blood. It was epic.'[15] What actions like this demonstrate is solidarity in the face of hardship, and the possibility of public recognition for political struggle. As Nell McCafferty wrote in the *Irish Times* (August 22, 1980): 'The menstrual blood on the walls of Armagh prison smells to high heaven. Shall we turn our noses up?'

Sweetness and light?

Very occasionally, prisoners in for politically motivated offences do not get *worse* treatment than other inmates, but *better*. There is often widespread support from people involved in their cause, sending in greetings from outside – and prison authorities may well be intrigued by the different nature of their offence, and be well disposed towards them, at least initially. (When the offence involves violence, or an immediate, serious threat to the state, this is unlikely.)

Pat Arrowsmith remembers one of her first sentences, in 1958 – thirty days in Holloway. She could see right away that there was a difference in treatment for the 'politicos'. 'Life was different for us because we got tons of Christmas cards and flowers. I think they sometimes relaxed the rules a bit with us over letting books and mail in, etc.'

Sometimes the authorities are devious enough to use political prisoners against the other women, to create hostility. Helen's friend, a Greenham woman, completed her sentence in Camberwell Police Station, because Holloway was completely full. Since plenty of women knew about her on the outside, she received a constant stream of gifts and visitors. Because the station was very crowded, the communal area – the only place where women could associate with each other, and have a smoke – was also the visiting room. Every time a visitor arrived, the women were sent back to their cells. Loretta had visits all the time... In addition, the police were obviously fond of her, and created a division which made Loretta, as well as the rest of the women, feel bad. As it was, resentment was already high, since part of the reason Holloway was so full was because it was jammed with Greenham women, all with relatively short sentences. The women were anxious to get into Holloway, and to have the prison facilities unavailable at a small police station.

Loretta soon felt that the privileges she was given were backhanded, and upsetting.

Just another prisoner?

Amid the extremes of treatment meted out to prisoners of conscience, lies the bland middle way, which is every government's public countenance. Words like 'criminal' and 'terrorist' conceal the unease which accompanies political activism of any kind, and countries all over the world would have us believe that all prisoners are just guilty, selfish women, and that the only injustice committed is the injustice of breaking the state's legal power.

In the Soviet Union political prisoners become psychiatric patients; in Latin America and Africa, activists in the Sandinistas and the ANC become 'terrorists', 'armed insurgents'; in Britain and Europe they just disappear. In *Decade*, a play by Jacki Holborough about Judith Ward, held in connection with Ireland, this ironic 'official statement' is uttered: 'This is England... There are no political prisoners here'. In Northern Ireland in 1976 Special Category Status, the tacit acceptance of political prisoners, was removed. We were now supposed to believe that there was nothing different about Republican prisoners. As the London Armagh Women's Group wrote in February 1984: 'Despite the fact that the British government refuses to grant these women political status, its excessively repressive treatment of them gives the lie to its insistence that they are "ordinary criminals".' And what, after all, is an 'ordinary criminal'?

MAKING THE CONNECTIONS: WE ARE ALL POLITICAL?

The lofty struggles of the political prisoner seem far removed from the more mundane every-day realities of women shoplifters, prostitutes and defrauders. It is the politicos who receive world wide attention and concern, who have Amnesty International campaigning to free them, and endless pickets and demonstrations in their support. But are these political women, conscious activists as they are, so far apart from their other sisters inside – the ones who carry the stigma of a 'criminal' label, the ones who are invisible in the shadow of their glory? There are many women, politicised while in prison on criminal charges, who resent the gulf created between those inside for the sake of an ideal, and those inside for the lack of an alternative. As Jenny Hicks says at the beginning of the chapter: all prisoners are in some way political. There may be a strategic need to proclaim political status, but we should also look underneath that term for its wider application – for the unity that goes deeper than the surface division.

What is politics anyway? It is about power: those who wield it, and those who suffer under it. It is when you go inside a prison – the political dustbin – that power structures underpinning a society really hit you between the eyes. What do you find in a women's prison? Lots of women who should never be there – not dangerous criminals, but women who cannot pay petty fines, or who lack the social contacts to get them out. Many Greenham protesters, often middle-class women, never inside before, have learned as much about politics from being in jail as they have during their political life outside. They have registered shock and dismay, not only at prison conditions, but at the reasons for women being there in the first place. Says one: 'The only crime that women in here have committed is that of not having enough money and influence to escape conviction.'[16]

For each of the reasons women gave in chapter 1 for committing crime, there is a link with what can also be spurs to political action: small and tenuous, but it's there. First, money. Criminals are regarded as 'greedy' – and, like the rest of humanity, some of them are. Others are in need. Others still, recognise a common need. Remember Mandy, who said: 'I'd be thieving for six families [on the housing estate], just like Robin Hood. And I know plenty who did that.' Second, anger: anger at general injustice as well as personal privation. Mandy again, talking about cheap dresses marked up by shop owners to an extortionate degree: 'The people who charge that amount are thieves already.' Third, success: a feeling of status, and achievement.

Fourth, kicks: the rush of adrenalin, the release of pent-up energy and frustration. Fifth, desperation. No other way to turn. Political activists will know about all these reasons for challenging the law.

One thing which is very striking when you meet women who have been involved in crime is their emotional integrity. For every one who is embittered, devious or self-obsessed – the traditional identikit picture of the criminal – there are two or three who have a deep awareness of what is happening to them, even if, through reasons of class, colour, articulacy or circumstance, they are unable to change it. Prison exists to cause pain. Sometimes, through that pain, comes acute perception. If you still labour under the misconception that women prisoners are pathetic failures, then forget it. You have more to learn than they have.

While writing this book, I was warned by a psychiatrist not to rely on the word of the women I interviewed, or else I would get a 'warped' view of the situation. I remain puzzled as to the alternative. Books? Experts? Statistics? Government ministers? He spoke of his criminalised clients amiably enough, but from a distance, from a high ladder looking down the rungs to the bottom. Some political activists regard other inmates in the same way. The process of learning to dispense with the ladder can itself be condescending, says Jenny Hicks: 'For them to come to terms with the fact that they are criminals in the same way as the woman who constantly goes out and shoplifts, or smashes the window to be arrested, is a form of academic or intellectual snobbery'.

Greenham women, through their persistent campaigning around the nuclear issue and regular imprisonment, have not only attracted publicity to conditions inside Holloway, but also have learned to make some important connections. Although Jenny Hicks is right when she suggests that some of these women do 'a tremendous amount of harm. They have no feeling for the rest of the women who haven't yet called themselves political prisoners', there are others who have come to some startling realisations. In *Greenham Common: Women At The Wire* one woman describes her own discovery: 'It was with horror I watched the pattern emerge. As a feminist I knew women were oppressed by men. As a feminist I knew nothing. I had gone to prison with the arrogant notion that we 36 Greenham women were political prisoners. After a few days I realised all 300 of us were political prisoners, and that the common link had a gender; it was male.'[17] As Chris Tchaikovsky of Women in Prison, says, 'I don't believe we are put inside for our crimes, but for rebelling against our feminity.' (see chapter 1) The Greenham campaign itself is now broadening out to include anti-apartheid actions and 'third world' politics. In the same way, the divide between what is 'political' and 'not political' is gradually closing. As Greenham woman Helen explains, 'Going into a supermarket and stealing food because you've got no money is as political as breaking into a nuclear base and saying "We don't want Cruise missiles".'

The difference between the two actions is often one of attitude. Political activists *consciously* commit certain crimes, acting from a set of beliefs, and often backed up by a group or organisation working for the same goals. An individual crime like shoplifting may be just as genuine a protest, and contain the same urgency as a 'political crime' – but the reasons are often *un*conscious, not thought through so well, even if felt as deeply. Political prisoners have the gift of optimism. They believe in a better world and will fight for it – often to the death. They have the luxury of an ideal. 'Ordinary' offenders are faced with a more negative alternative. They may not have found support from anyone else, or have been exposed to any philosophy other than that of survival. They are often fierce pragmatists, struggling *against* an unfair system, rather than *for* a brighter alternative. There is no need to denigrate either battle. As Jenny Hicks says, 'You're all in (prison) for different reasons.' In the end there is nothing romantic about the repression of prison. The least we on the outside can do is to educate ourselves about crime and punishment, and learn what it is like to be locked up. Prison is a very powerful symbol of a country's humanitarian values – or lack of them. We cannot afford to remain ignorant. Above all, it is important to listen to women who commit crime – those hidden, ignored, despised people, who deserve our attention as much as everybody else. There are extraordinary, deep divisions between criminal and non-criminal women, between 'political' and 'ordinary' prisoners, between those labelled 'bad', and those stigmatised still further as 'mad'. Everybody loves a label – it makes the non-labelled among us feel safe. But labels and divisions solve nothing. If there is one thing I have learned while researching this book, it is the undoubted strength of all the women I have spoken to, and their ability to see where they have 'gone wrong' – and where society has gone wrong with them. Tapped in a more creative and beneficial way, that strength could help us all grow, away from the false and fierce divisions we so venomously cling to at present to a deeper, more understanding whole. Just remember the revolutionary words of Ho Chi Minh: 'When the gates of the prison are opened, the real dragon will fly out.'[18]

AFTERWORD

It is highly unlikely that the gates of prisons all round the world, housing women who have committed all manner of crimes, will miraculously open one day and let them all go free. So when people ask, 'What should we do about prisons?' the answer 'Close them down!' is impractical, if tempting! There *are* women inside who are a danger to themselves and to others. Whether prison or psychiatric hospital is an appropriate place for them is debatable. But given the present political climate, suitable alternatives are unlikely to pop up and wipe away all those tears, all those lost years.

So what can we do? If we are to believe some criminologists, who suggest that 'nothing works', that crime is simply growing, and recidivism is an unalterable fact of life, then we will do nothing – except maybe increase the penalties, enforce the punishment, and shut our eyes. But is there an alternative? There is. I found, while writing this book, that there is a wealth of information forthcoming about the nature of crime – why it happens and what it means – available from source: from the women who commit it. One of the first steps towards breaking down public prejudice and fear is to listen to these women. Visit them in prison. Talk to friends who have been involved in crime. Join campaigning groups like Women In Prison. Facts are startling. But false assumptions are deadly. There is a grey fog of misleading information which surrounds the whole area of women and crime, a fog made murkier by official secrecy and media scares, but one which it would be very easy to blow away.

The meanness of spirit which surrounds the Home Office in Britain – a public institution after all, and one which presides over our collective penal system – is extraordinarily counterproductive. Way back at the beginning of my research, when I was still pretty optimistic (and naïve) about the restrictions on crime and prison reporting, I rang the Home Office to try and arrange an interview with the then governor of Holloway, Joy Kinsley. The brisk voice at the end of the phone asked me to put my request in writing, including a list of the questions I wanted to ask. I did so. A week later the owner of the same brisk voice rang me back. 'I'm afraid the governor will not have time to see you.' When I protested that it would be a great pity to write a book about women and crime and not have *any* contact with the prison governor (I later went to hear Kinsley's successor speak at a public meeting), he replied, 'Oh, I don't know that it's necessary. I mean, one of the questions you ask in your letter is "Why do you think women commit crime?" The answer is quite simple. *Greed.*' With that one word he wiped out the liberal intentions of a century of penal reform, and many more centuries of struggle by criminalised women themselves. There must be a more open, creative alternative to this. The media has a duty to explore it; the government must back such open investigation – and individuals must do *their* bit to educate themselves on the reality behind such a reactionary facade.

Something which must accompany a more open attitude to the subject is the breaking down of false divisions between different women. As chapters 1 and 6 suggest, the categories of 'ordinary' (that is, non-criminalised) women, the 'criminal', and the 'political prisoner', suggest rigid differences, and a hierarchy between the 'good', the 'bad', and the 'committed' female. These definitions mask a more blurred and muddled reality. Some criminal women have become highly politicised during their prison sentences, and rightfully resent the elitism of political campaigners who insist on a privileged status away from the main prison population. *All* criminalised women suffer from the stigma of not fulfilling their traditional delegated role as pure and moral peacemaker – keeper of all laws, inside and outside the home.

The role of women is changing rapidly, in all areas of everyday life, with the increased and persistent influence of feminism; but feminists too have been slow to look at the criminal culture and how it affects women. It has taken the initiatives of ex-prisoners themselves to really draw attention to the sexual discrimination of the law and prisons. The way women are treated when arrested is highly symbolic – in a dramatically heightened way – of most women's predicament.

Women who do not carry the 'criminal' label can learn from the prison experience of other women. They all have more in common than they may think: sexual harassment; stereotyping; patronising and humiliating assumptions about their 'fitness' as wives and mothers; physical degradation; psychological aggression; isolation; conflicting messages about how to behave; boredom within a limited, restricted lifestyle.

Even if we do start to understand *why* crime occurs – and possibly help to stop harmful patterns being set up in some women's lives, by providing material or emotional support before they even commit a crime – the flow of lives in through those prison gates will undoubtedly continue.

Prison is unpleasant. It is an extreme form of punishment, and the regime of prison is an added humiliation. Some would argue that the loss of liberty is itself punishment enough. Why make it worse, and make the prisoner *more* hardened and embittered than ever, when rehabilitation within prison walls may stop the prisoner ever offending again? British pressure group Women in Prison has campaigned consistently for improvements within the penal system. The measures they call for are humane ones: the increase of personal contact between the prisoner and her friends, family and other prisoners; improved medical facilities to replace the prevailing, pop-a-pill mentality; the removal of reporting restrictions imposed in Britain by the Official Secrets Act and overseas by its equivalents; and increased funding for non-custodial alternatives to prison, such as community service and sheltered housing. The impetus behind these demands public accountability. We need frankness in the face of a problem which affects us all, and which is not helped by government secrecy and obfuscation.

The only way to stop crime is to give its instigators a more creative alternative, which means encouraging a woman's innate independence, and the pursuit of practical and artistic skills which reflect her talents in a more publicly acceptable manner than do shoplifting or fraud. Teaching her how to be a 'good wife and mother' – the rationale behind much of the old-style prison thinking – is not going to create a dynamic new way of life, and besides alienating single women, as well as many married ones, may even encourage the old pain and passivity which provoked criminal action in the first place.

But the best prison facilities in the world will stand for nothing if there is no backup when women emerge, having served their sentence, into open society. Despite the valiant efforts of probation officers, social workers, women's hostels, employment and advice services, there is still a vast lack – in Britain at least – of adequate support for ex-prisoners. Not only do they have emotional and psychological adjustments to make, but they also face complex problems to do with benefits, housing and work. The complexities created by prison – the deprivation and its after-effects – are massive. Often the most important immediate comfort is to talk to someone who has been through a similar experience; and so organisationas run by ex-prisoners themselves are particularly vital. Women in Prison, Clean Break Theatre, and the Creative and Supportive Trust (see chapter 2) create positive alternatives for criminalised women – and help to publicise their lives in an original, realistic way. But these organisations struggle to survive financially, relying on grants which are in short supply. Why does the government not supply direct funding to establish more such groups up and down the country? Do we want to encourage the individual intelligence and autonomy of women? Or do we prefer spending over £400 per prisoner per week of our taxes on keeping them behind locked doors?

It is easy to just shout for money (though this sort of strategy will undoubtedly *save* money in the end, and it will certainly save our lives – from misery and anger). But money is not the underlying problem. The real stumbling block is in our hearts and minds. How many of us can admit to harbouring no prejudice against criminalised women? Who can honestly say they do *not* read the gutter press reports on Myra Hindley or some other suspected woman murderer, or on prostitution, and get a little thrill from the awful exotic titillation of the story? It lies buried very deep, the attitude of prurience, fear and loathing towards the criminal woman – and indeed towards any woman who does the unexpected, the unfeminine: the unforgivable. We have to look at that hidden horror before we can change anything with conviction, and for the good. For many 'criminal' women it is already too late. Whose fault? Theirs?

Notes

Chapter 1   Why did she do it?

1   *A Dictionary of Criminology*, Dermot Walsh and Adrian Poole (Routledge & Kegan Paul, 1983).

2   NACRO report, 1978

3   'The female offender as an object of criminological research', Christine Rasche in *The Female Offender*, ed. Annette Brodsky (Sage Publications, USA, 1975).

4   *Prostitutes: Our Life*, ed. Claude Jaget (Falling Wall Press, 1980).

5   *Ibid.*

6   *Sisters in Crime*, Freda Adler (McGraw Hill, USA, 1975).

7   *Women, Crime and Criminology*, Carol Smart (Routledge & Kegan Paul, 1976).

8   *Controlling Women: The Normal and the Deviant*, Bridget Hutter and Gillian Williams (Croom Helm, 1981).

9   *Prostitutes: Our Life*.

10   *Ibid.*

11   Cecil Bishop, quoted in Carol Smart, *Women, Crime and Criminology*.

12   *Prostitutes: Our Life*.

13 *Woman at Point Zero*, Nawal El Saadawi (Zed Press, 1983).

14 *Prostitutes: Our Life.*

15 *Criminal Women*, ed. Pat Carlen (Polity Press, 1985).

16 *Women's Imprisonment*, Pat Carlen (Routledge & Kegan Paul, 1983).

17 *Prostitutes: Our Life.*

18 Introduction to *Blood Relations* by Sharon Pollock, in *Plays by Women*, ed. Michelene Wandor (Methuen, 1984).

Chapter 2   Paying for it: Police, the law, the courts.

1 *An Aboriginal Mother Tells of the Old and the New*, Labumore, Elsie Roughsey (Penguin, Australia, 1984).

2 *Law: The Old and the New: Aboriginal Women in Central Australia Speak Out*, Diane Bell and Pam Ditton (Central Australian Aboriginal Legal Aid Service, 1980).

3 *Not In God's Image: Women In History*, ed. Julia O'Faolain and Lauro Martines (Virago, 1979).

4 *Ibid.*

5 *Ibid.*

6 *Ibid.*

7 'Women and Policing In London', GLC Police Committee Support Unit, Issue 3, November 1985.

8 *Girls will be Girls; Sexism and Juvenile Justice in a London Borough*, Maggie Casburn (Women's Research and Resources Centre, Explorations in Feminism, 1979).

9 *Ibid.*

10 'Female delinquency and social reaction', Lesley Smith (Women and Deviancy Conference, Essex University, April 1975).

11 Barbara Hudson writing in *Community Care* (April 4, 1985).

12 Mentioned in *Cosmopolitan* magazine (February 1984). 'Live Issues', p. 42.

13 *Women in the Penal System*, Baroness Seear and Elaine Player (Howard League for Penal Reform, January 1986).

14 *Women On Trial*, Susan Edwards (Manchester University Press, 1984).

15 *The Adolescent Girl in Conflict*, Gisela Konopka (Prentice Hall, New Jersey, 1966).

Chapter 3   Going Down: Prison Walls

1   *The Pain of Confinement*, Jimmy Boyle (Pan Books, 1985).

2   *Women and Russia*, ed. Tatiana Mamanova (Basil Blackwell, 1985).

3   *Women's Imprisonment*, Pat Carlen (Routledge & Kegan Paul, 1983).

4   *A Woman in Custody*, Audrey Peckham (Fontana, 1985).

5   Marilyn Haft in *Women, Crime and Justice*, eds Susan K. Datesman and Frank R. Scarpitti (Oxford University Press, 1980).

6   *Women in the Penal System*, Baroness Seear and Elaine Player (Howard League for Penal Reform, January 1986).

7   Figures provided by Women in Prison campaign.

8   Telecea in *This Place*, Andrea Freud Loewenstein (Pandora, 1985).

Chapter 4   Madness and crime: The doomed search for potency

1   Information from Carol Smart's book, *Women, Crime and Criminology* (Routledge & Kegan Paul, 1976).

2   Statistics from HMSO *Criminal Statistics for England and Wales*, 1981, and DHSS *In-Patient Statistics from the Mental Health Enquiry for England*, 1981.

3   From information in *Women and Madness*, Phyllis Chesler (Avon, 1972).

4   *And I Don't Want to Live This Life*, Deborah Spungen (Corgi, 1984).

5   Quoted in MIND's *Evidence to Government Select Committee on PMS*, 1985, Great Britain.

6   *Women and the Psychiatric Paradox*, P. Susan Penfold and Gillian A. Walker (Open University Press, 1984).

7   *Women, Crime and Criminology*.

8   'Medicine and murderous women in the mid-nineteenth century', Roger Smith, paper given at Social History Conference on 'Crime, Violence and Social Protest', Birmingham, January 1977.

9   *Women and Madness*.

10   Christine English drove a car at her lover after discovering his infidelity. She pleaded, and was found guilty of manslaughter on the grounds of diminished responsibility due to PMS.

11   See note 7.

12   *And I Don't Want to Live This Life*.

13   *The Bell Jar*, Sylvia Plath (Faber, 1966).

14   *Ibid.*

15   *Faces in the Water*, Janet Frame (Women's Press, 1980).

16   *Women and Madness*.

17   *And I Don't Want to Live This Life*.

18   *The Madness of a Seduced Woman*, Susan Fromberg Schaeffer (Pan, 1985).

19   *The Silent Twins*, Marjorie Wallace (Chatto & Windus, 1986).

20   Women in Mental Health can be contacted via A Woman's Place, Hungerford House, Victoria Embankment, London WC2. Tel. 01–836 6081.

21   *Too Much Anger, Too Much Pain*, Janet and Paul Gotkin (Jonathan Cape, 1977).

Chapter 5   Trial by media: Popular images of women and crime

1   Colin MacInnes, from *Absolute MacInnes* (Allison & Busby, 1985), quote taken from article on 'The Criminal Society', *The Spectator*, December 1961.

2   Article by Jane Root: 'Inside!', *The Abolitionist*, number 10, Winter 1982.

3   *In the Underworld*, Laurie Taylor (Counterpoint/George Allen & Unwin, 1985).

4   Article by Pratibha Parmar: 'Hateful contraries', *Ten 8*, number 16, 1984.

5   *Women who Kill*, Ann Jones (Holt, Rinehart & Winston, Canada, 1980).

6   *Gyn/Ecology*, Mary Daly (Women's Press, 1979).

7   *Victorian Murderesses*, Mary S. Hartman (Robson Books, 1985).

8   Article by Chris Auty: 'The bravest woman I ever hanged', *City Limits*, February 22, 1985.

9   *Ruth Ellis: The Last Woman to be Hanged*, Robert Hancock (Weidenfeld & Nicolson, 1985).

10   Article by Gillian Skirrow: 'Euston Films Ltd' in *Made for Television*, ed. Manuel Alvarado and John Stewart (Thames/Methuen, 1985).

11   *Any Four Women Could Rob the Bank of Italy*, Ann Cornelisen (Penguin, 1985).

12   *Moll Cutpurse*, Ellen Galford (Stramullion, 1984).

13   *A Woman in Custody*, Audrey Peckham (Fontana, 1985).

14   *Criminal Women*, ed. Pat Carlen (Polity Press, 1985).

15   *And I Don't Want to Live This Life*, Deborah Spungen (Corgi, 1984).

16   *Woman at Point Zero*, Nawal El Saadawi (Zed Press, 1983).

Chapter 6   The political connection

1   *I Think of My Mother: Claudia Jones*, Buzz Johnson (Karia Press, 1985).

2   *A Dictionary of Criminology*, Dermot Walsh and Adrian Poole (Routledge & Kegan Paul, 1983).

3   *The Making of Tania*, David Boulton (New English Library, 1975).

4   *If They Come in the Morning*, Angela Davis (Orbach & Chambers, 1971).

5   *SCUM Manifesto*, Valerie Solanas (Matriarchy Study Groups, 1983).

6   *Greenham Common: Women at the Wire*, eds Barbara Harford and Sarah Hopkins (Women's Press, 1984).

7   *Hitler's Children*, Jillian Becker (Granada, 1978).

8   *Woman at Point Zero*, Nawal El Saadawi (Zed Press, 1983).

9   'Stripsearches in Armagh Jail' (London Armagh Women's Group, February 1984).

10   *Irish Feminist Review* (Women's Community Press, 1984).

11   *Ibid.*

12   *Ibid.*

13   *Kiss of the Spiderwoman*, Manuel Puig (Arena, 1984).

14   *Ibid.*

15   *Tell them Everything*, Margaretta D'Arcy (Pluto Press, 1981).

16   *Greenham Common: Women at the Wire*.

17   *Ibid.*

18   *Vida*, Marge Piercy (Women's Press, 1980). A novel about an American radical on the run from the police.

GOOD BOOKS AND USEFUL ADDRESSES

1   *A Dictionary of Criminology*, Dermot Walsh and Adrian Poole (Routledge & Kegan Paul, 1983). Useful catalogue of jargon which is used in the study of crime; what it means and how it is applied.

2   *And I Don't Want to Live This Life*, Deborah Spungen (Corgi, 1984). A harrowing and moving account by Nancy Spungen's mother, of how her daughter got involved in drugs, rock'n roll and disaster. Really revealing about press harassment and smear tactics, as well as showing how different the truth is from the social misconceptions which surround women who will not conform to traditional stereotypes.

3   *Any Four Women Could Rob the Bank of Italy*, Ann Cornelisen (Penguin, 1983). A very amusing romp.

4   **Apex Trust**, 31–33 Clapham Road, London SW9. Telephone: 01-582 3171. Set up in 1965 to help ex-prisoners with employment problems. They now also focus on the long-term unemployed, and on the particular needs of women ex-prisoners.

5 *A Woman in Custody*, Audrey Peckham (Fontana, 1985). A first-hand account of one woman's experience of being remanded in custody on charges of 'incitement to murder'. Useful because it is based on personal experience, but some of the author's attitudes towards other women in the remand centre are worryingly condescending.

6 **Black Female Prisoners' Scheme**, 141 Stockwell Road, London SW9. Telephone 01-733 5520. Advice and information for black women ex-prisoners. Also a pressure group aiming to publicise the particular discrimination faced by black criminalised women.

7 **Clean Break Theatre**. Same address as CAST above. Set up by ex-prisoners Jenny Hicks and Jacki Holborough, while they were in open prison, and has been touring since 1979. The group gives workshops for and performances by women ex-prisoners. It has links with Holloway, as well as being highly respected in the arts world for its professional productions, centring around the experience of women, crime and prison.

8 **Creative and Supportive Trust**, 34a Stratford Villas, London NW1. Telephone: 01-485 0367. This was set up in 1982 by ex-prisoner Lennie Spear, and provides training workshops to develop practical and creative skills, from photography to dressmaking, with a view to job creation or self-employment.

9 *Criminal Women*, P. Carlen, J. Hicks, J. O'Dwyer, D. Christina, C. Tchaikovsky (Polity Press, 1985). Invaluable first-hand accounts of women and crime. Very powerful, very political. Read this, if you read nothing else on the subject.

10 *Greenham Common: Women at the Wire*, edited by Barbara Harford and Sarah Hopkins (Women's Press, 1984). The politics of the Greenham movement, as well as excerpts from trials, and newspaper reports.

11 **Howard League for Penal Reform**, 322 Kennington Park

Road, London SE11. Telephone: 01-735 3317. As its name suggests, an organisation pushing for reform within the British penal system.

12   *If They Come In The Morning*, Angela Davis (Orbach & Chambers, 1971). Classic account by black American activist Angela Davis about her involvement in the radical black movement started in the 1960s, including her arrest and imprisonment.

13   *In Darkest London*, Mrs Cecil Chesterton (Stanley Paul, 1928). Interesting, if you can get hold of this in a library, to see the attitudes of middle-class reformers at the turn of the century. Her views are often very sensitive and surprisingly radical. Also gives a startling taste of life for the 'down and out' woman sixty years ago.

14   *In The Underworld*, Laurie Taylor (Counterpoint/Unwin, 1985). Not about women, but useful as a short reminder of how men form their own cliquey subculture around crime – making cosy clubs out of something which for women is just plain stigma. Laurie Taylor revels in it!

15   *Moll Cutpurse*, Ellen Galford (Stramullion, 1984). Absolutely delightful Elizabethan spoof about one legendary thief and 'naughty girl', Moll Cutpurse. Affectionate, ribald, and invigorating. At last a *heroine* of the underworld!

16   *NACRO (National Association for the Care and Rehabilitation of Offenders)*, 169 Clapham Road, London SW9 0PU. Telephone: 01-582 6500. Home Office-funded organisation. Useful for facts and figures about women and crime.

17   *Notes From A Waiting Room*, Alan Reeve (Heretic Books, 1983). Not about female experience – but useful insight into one man's struggle towards a political perception of his criminal life. Powerful.

18   **Prisoners' Advice and Information Network**, BM-PAIN, London WC1N 3XX. Set up by several different organisations to deal

with inquiries from prisoners or families regarding their treatment as prisoners. PAIN includes PROP – the National Prisoners' movement.

19 *Prostitutes: Our Life*, edited by Claude Jaget (Falling Wall Press, 1980). Very valuable first-hand accounts by prostitute women in France, telling it like it is – not how men would like it to seem.

20 **Radical Alternatives to Prison**, BCM Box 4842, London WC1N 3XX. 'If the aim of prison is to stop a person from committing crimes, there's no evidence that it works.' RAP's purpose is to promote radical alternatives to existing penal policies, and to 'challenge the myths and deceptions that support these policies'. They produce a useful magazine, *The Abolitionist*, several times a year, and provide lots of inside information about abuses within the penal system.

21 *Tell Them Everything*, Margaretta D'Arcy (Pluto Press, 1981). Account of the author's three month 'stay' in Armagh Jail on the no-wash protest. Grim reminder of prison reality for Republican women prisoners in the North of Ireland.

22 *The Pain of Confinement*, Jimmy Boyle (Pan 1985). Useful contrast to *A Woman In Custody*, giving the inside feelings and experiences of a man once dubbed 'Scotland's most violent man', and now an articulate and much-respected campaigner, with his own centre for ex-prisoner and drug users, the Gateway Exchange in Edinburgh.

23 *The Silent Twins*, Marjorie Wallace (Chatto & Windus, 1986). The extraordinary story of two black twin girls who refused to speak to anyone but each other from childhood, and who turned towards crime in frustration at the lack of outlet for their creative abilities. Both are writers, but have now landed up in Broadmoor, where their copious diary and story writing has apparently dried up.

24 *This Place*, Andrea Freud Loewenstein (Pandora, 1984). Big, powerful novel about four women in prison in America – two inmates and two therapists.

25   *Women and Crime*, Frances Heidensohn (Macmillan, 1985). Useful lucky bag of popular theories on women and crime. Academic rather than direct quotes from criminal women themselves.

26   *Women and Madness*, Phyllis Chesler (Avon Books, 1972). Seminal work on social and psychiatric abuse of women. Heavy going, but invaluable.

27   *Woman at Point Zero*, Nawal El Saadawi (Zed Books, 1983). Don't miss this one. Saadawi's account (based on fact) of one woman's life as she awaits execution for murdering her pimp, is not just a searing indictment of a world which creates prostitution and then enslaves women to it, but is a highly political analysis of women and men and the real nature of crime.

28   *Women, Crime and Criminology*, Carol Smart (Routledge & Kegan Paul, 1976). Highly academic analysis of male-dominated criminology and the harm it has done to women.

29   **Women Prisoners' Resource Centre**, Room One, 1 Thorpe Close, Ladbroke Grove, London W10 5XL. Telephone: 01-968 3121. NACRO-backed referral centre for women in custody, or just released, in London.

30   **Women in Prison**, 444 Chiswick High Road, London W4. Telephone: 01-994 6470/1. Fantastically energetic and powerful pressure group set up by ex-prisoner Chris Tchaikovsky in the early 1980s, WIP works not only to publicise conditions for women prisoners but to effect change within the prison system itself.

31   *Women On Trial*, Susan S. M. Edwards (Manchester University Press, 1984). Academic but useful research into the way the female suspect is treated by the legal and penal system in Britain.

32   *Women's Imprisonment*, Pat Carlen (Routledge & Kegan Paul, 1983). Useful research into women in prison in Scotland. Lots of quotes from the women inmates themselves, and humane, feminist analysis.

33 *Worlds Apart: Women Under Immigration and Nationality Law*, Women, Immigration and Nationality Group (Pluto Press, 1985). Guide to the particular iniquities of Britain's immigration policies, how it makes criminals out of women who have committed no crime. The wider subject is racism and the law.

INDEX